SWISS MOUNTAIN RAI

Vol 1 - AROUND LUZERN AND IN

With an introduction to rack systems and

PHILIP J.KELLEY DONALD BINNS

New in 1992, Brienz Rothorn Bahn No.12 was photographed descending with a two-coach train in its home surroundings. Note the front top-end compartment for the use of the conductor. *Chr.Lüber, Brienz via SLM, Winterthur*

Designed by Donald Binns
Published and type-set by Trackside Publications, 50 Long Meadow, Skipton, North Yorkshire, England, BD23 1BW.
Printed by Amadeus Press Ltd, 517 Leeds Road, Huddersfield, West Yorkshire, HD2 1YJ

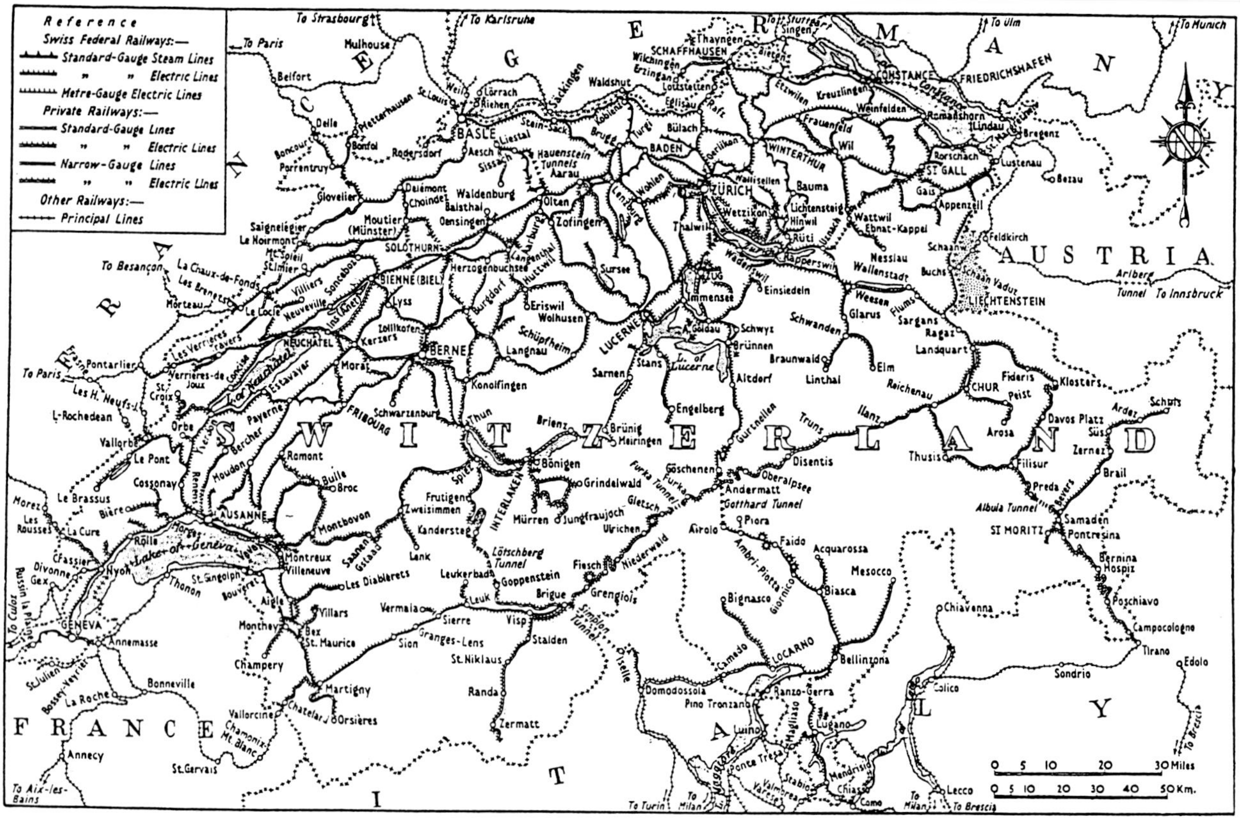

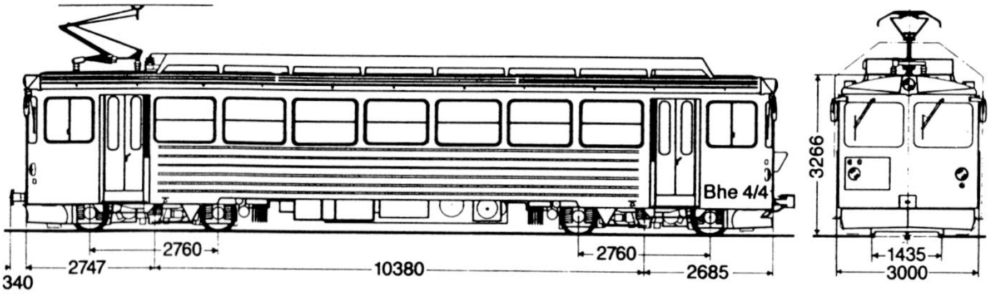

SWISS MOUNTAIN RAILWAYS Vol 1 - AROUND LUZERN AND INTERLAKEN

Philip J.Kelley

Donald Binns

First Published 5/1999

CONTENTS

INTRODUCTION

Originally the idea behind this book was to convey, by means of photographs, how things looked thirty and forty years ago on the Swiss narrow gauge. Many of the pictures were taken in the 1950s, others in 1967. During this period many of the older vehicles were about to be replaced by new stock, in many instances the old and new were running side by side. Some of the lines were pure adhesion, others rack and adhesion, others rack only.

The Swiss realised right from the start that their scenery was superb and it was very important to enable their own people and latterly tourists to be able to travel extensively. Even today it is recognised that it is vitally important to be able to maintain communications by rail, especially in the winter months.

The technical achievement in getting some of the lines to the top of the mountains is really incredible considering the terrain involved. In many cases instead of using rack and adhesion systems(or rack only), funicular or air cableway has been adopted. We have included some typical funiculars in this book.

At this stage our Publisher was perfectly happy to go ahead but suggested that perhaps the book could be worked up to consider the Swiss mountain railways and their locomotives in detail along with a brief history introducing the different forms of rack systems and their locomotives. Additional information was added along with historic postcard reproductions, more steam locomotive photographs and drawings, plus early electric locomotive drawings and builders details. The finished result will it is hoped give readers a better insight into Swiss mountain railways from early times to the present. The final chapter brings the story up-to-date with details of the new rack steam locomotives built by SLM.

The outcome was a mass of information - much more than could be used in one book without increasing the price to a level which would restrict sales. Accordingly it was decided to produce two seperate books. In this first volume we look at the early years of rack railways along with types and locomotives, then we consider mountain railways around Luzern, followed by those around Interlaken. Our final chapter looks at the new H2/3 rack locomotive built by SLM, Winterthur. Volume 2 will be divided into geographical areas with an area sketch map at the start of each chapter. Both books are comprehensive but do not claim to be complete. In addition to the railways and funiculars presented there were and are other railways, tramways and funiculars which could have been included.

Most mountain railways around Luzern and Interlaken have been covered with a few typical examples of funicular railways, but although a perfectly respectable way of climbing mountains, cable-cars do not run on rails and therefore are excluded. In the original plan it was intended to include a brief selection of tramways that were extant in the 1950/1960s and although nothing to do with Mountain railways these are included as a bonus. A good number have been replaced by trolleybuses, or motorbuses or have been closed together.

P.J.Kelley D.Binns

ACKNOWLEDGEMENTS

I would like to thank the Railway Gazette for permission to reproduce one of their maps in this book. I would also like to thank Mr Henry Ernst, who was Manager of the London office of the Swiss National Tourist Office and the Swiss Federal Railways during the time of the Authors' early visits to Switzerland; his help in arranging specal visists and footplate passes is very much appreciated. Also many thanks to the many railway staff in Switzerland who went out of their way to explain and answer many of the writers' questions, to them I dedicate this book.

Very many thanks also to Donald Binns of Trackside Publications for his encouragement throughout.

P.J.Kelley

PUBLISHERS ACKNOWLEDGEMENTS

I would like to thank the Swiss railways who have supplied much information for use in this book and particulary the Pilatusbahn and the Rigibahn. Their generosity in allowing use of their material is much appreciated.

Donald Binns

Outside front cover: Wengernalp Bahnen Railcar BCFhe 4/4 No.105 built by SLM, Works No.4045/1950, was photographed on a train at Laüterbrunnen on 1 June 1955. *P.J.Kelley*

Outside back cover: Stansstad-Engelbergbahn railcar ABFZe 3/4 No.9 was photographed arriving at Stansstad on 15 June 1956. *P.J.Kelley*

On the Brünigbahn the 09.11am train from Giswil to Luzern was photographed at Hergiswil on 25 May 1954 headed by Fhe 4/6 Gepack - Triebwagen(motor luggage van)No.908. This one metre gauge unit was built by SLM, Works No.3729/1941, and is fitted with seperate adhesion and rack drive bogies. Maximum speed on the adhesion section is 75km/hr and on the rack 33km/hr. The adhesion motors also work on the rack sections but with reduced voltage.

P.J.Kelley

On the Brienz Rothorn Bahn 1996 built No.12 was photographed with Lake Brienz in the back-ground.

SLM, Winterthur

AN INTRODUCTION TO RACK RAILWAYS AND THEIR LOCOMOTIVES

1

EARLY YEARS

When thinking of rack railways Switzerland immediately springs to mind along with the 'Schweizerischen Lokomotiv und Maschinenfabrik (SLM)'whose Winterthur works have built a high proportion of the worlds rack locomotives. Indeed rack railways are to be found in many parts of the world, but the type is linked inextricably with Switzerland, although the honour of a 'first' goes to England. Within this volume will be found many references to Swiss rack railways powered by steam and/or electric locomotives, and whilst only covering those lines within the Luzern and Interlaken areas, it is hoped to produce a second volume looking at the rest of Switzerland. This survey looks at both narrow and standard gauge railways starting with the two 4ft 8½in gauge rack railways on the Rigi.These of course occupy a special place in the development of the type - the Vitznau-Rigi being the first European rack railway open for passenger traffic. The idea of using a locomotive fitted with a toothed gear wheel engaging with a rack laid between the ordinary rails, for climbing steep grades, is almost as old as the locomotive itself.

The first known rack-railway locomotive was tried out on 12 August 1811 on the Middleton colliery railway, Leeds(England). In this instance it was not a case of climbing steep gradients and at that time John Blenkinsop did not know that the friction between the rail and the wheel was enough to provide for the progress of the locomotive and the traction of the train. In his system the rack was located outside the running rails. A six-wheel locomotive with gearing for working in a rack was built by the Neath Abbey Works, South Wales for the Dowlais Iron Company in 1836. This was probably the first ever locomotive to be fitted for combined rack and adhesion working and was specially intended for steep gradients. Its cylinders were inclined; the connecting rods being coupled to cranks on a shaft located under the back end of the boiler. Power was transmitted from this shaft to the trailing coupled axle by means of gearing, and was also connected by gearing with a shaft carrying the cranks for working the valves and with another shaft on whch was mounted the large

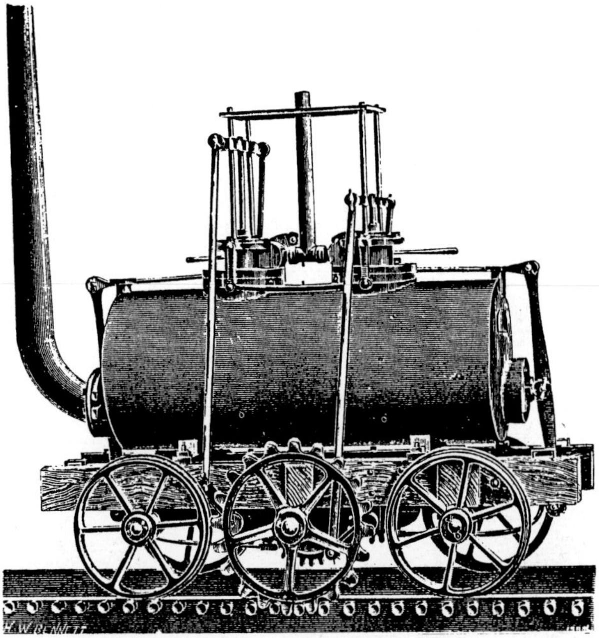

The Middleton Colliery rack locomotive of 1811.
"Engineer"

pinion which geared into the rack. An arrangement was provided for lifting this pinion out of gear with the rack, when required.

In America in 1831 Rimber proposed placing a rack in the centre between the two rails, and this idea was carried out by Cathcart in 1847 when a rack section between the running rails was laid on the 1 in 16⅔ Madison Incline of the Jeffersonville, Madison & Indianapolis Railway. This incline was first worked by horses but in 1848 the Baldwin Locomotive Works(USA)built a combined rack/adhesion locomotive to plans patented by Andrew Cathcart(Master Mechanic of the J.M.& I.R.). The locomotive had 8 adhesion driving wheels 3ft 6in diameter, with power transmitted from a pair of outside inclined cylinders to the third axle. A second pair of cylinders was mounted vertically at either side of the boiler and transmitted power to a crankshaft under the boiler and between the 2nd and 3rd pair of driving wheels. A single cog wheel was mounted centrally on this crankshaft and engaged with another twice its

Diagram of Baldwin rack/adhesion 0-8-0T supplied in 1848 to the Jeffersonville, Madison & Indianapolis Railway. D.Binns collection

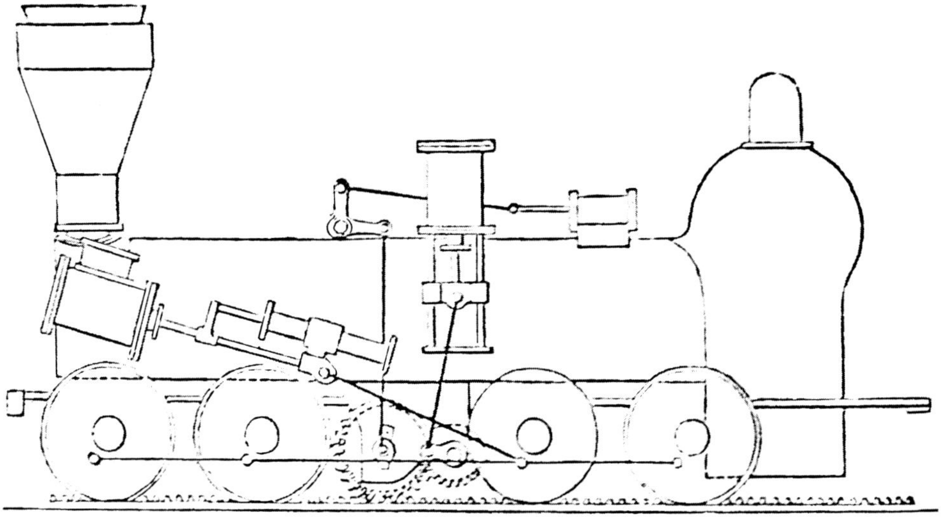

The six-wheel locomotive with rack gearing built by the Neath Abbey Works for the Dowlais Iron Company in 1836.

The "Rebuen Wells" 0-10-0T was built in 1868 as a replacement for the two Baldwin rack/adhesion 0-8-0T pictured at the top of this page. "Engineer"

diameter on a second shaft immediately in front, this latter engaging with a rack-rail placed centrally between the tracks. The inclined cylinders transmitted power to the 8 wheels on the adhesion sections of the railway whilst the vertical cylinders powered the rack mechanism. By means of a steam cylinder the rack gear wheel could be raised or lowered as required to engage with or disengage from the rack. The rack itself, was 10in wide and the teeth had a pitch of 4in.

The locomotive weighing "upwards of 30 tons" proved satisfactory, so much so that a second one was built by Baldwin in 1851. These carried the names *"John Bright"* and *"John Brough"*. The pair of Baldwin rack/adhesion locomotives continued to work the line until July 1868 when Reuben Wells(the Locomotive Superintendent) built in the Company shops at Jeffersonville a "special grade climbing locomotive" with 5 pairs of 3ft 8in driving wheels placed in two groups, 3 pairs infront of the firebox and 2 pairs behind, but all coupled by a long side-rod(presumably with some degree of flexibility built in). A pair of outside cylinders 20in x 24in were mounted at the front and drove onto the third axle. The boiler was 4ft 8in diameter and contained 201 tubes 12ft long x 2in diameter. Water(1800 gallons)was carried in two unusual cylindrical tanks each 26ft long x 2ft 5in diameter located above the ten driving wheels. Another unusual feature was a track brake(or sled)but unfortunately your Authors do not know how this worked. The total weight of this 0-10-0T was 112,000lb, the whole being available for adhesion.

The *"Reuben Wells"* successfully worked the incline by adhesion for many years and it was withdrawn when the line was acquired by the Pennsylvania Railroad who had more powerful locomotives readily available. It was then presented to the Purdue University Railway Museum where it remained for many years. Eventually, however, it was returned to the Pennsylvania Railroad and in 1968 was given to the Children's Museum, in Indianapolis, Indiana.

The first person to conquer a mountain proper was a retired businessman named Sylvester Marsh, a practical inventor of devices for the food processing business. He became interested in the problems of building a steam railroad capable of climbing a mountain. In 1857 he applied to the State of New Hampshire(USA)for a charter to build a rack railway up Mount Washington 6288ft above sea level(in the White Mountains). At that time people thought his ideas were lunacy and his proposal was not favoured. It was not until after the American Civil War that he found investors and by that time the New Hampshire Legislature had approved the project. The Mount Washington Cog Railway opened in

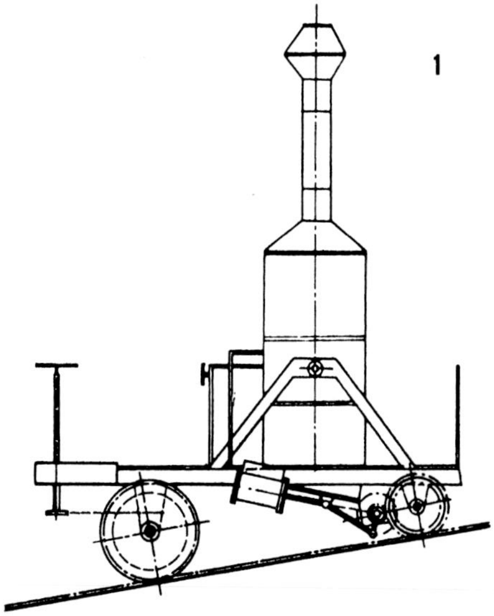
1

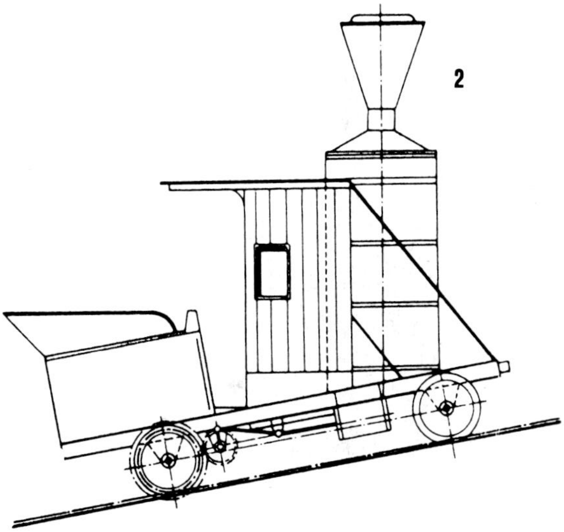
2

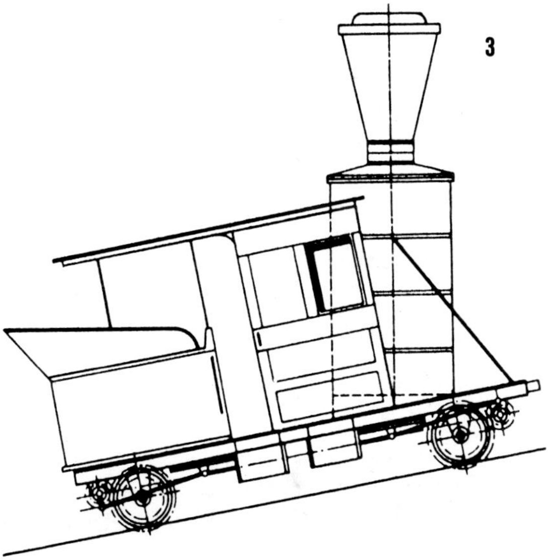
3

The drawings on pages 7 and 8 represent different designs of rack locomotives for the Mount Washington Railway. The line was opened in 1869 but No.1 "Hero"("Peppersass"), had been built in 1866 by Campbell, Whittier & Co., Cambridgeport, Mass, USA. Second No.3 "Hercules" was the first MWR locomotive to be built new with a horizontal boiler and No.1 was to be the last of the vertical boiler locomotives to survive, being replaced in 1878. The second drawing depicts a vertical boiler locomotive with the cylinders and drive reversed. The third drawing shows an early design of four-wheel locomotive with four cylinders and vertical boiler, whilst drawing four depicts No.9 of 1908 with horizontal boiler and four cylinder layout, plus seperate four-wheel tender. Most Mount Washington Railway locomotives were built by the Manchester Locomotive Works, Manchester, USA. The types are illustrated since the Vitznau-Rigi locomotives were developed from these following Niklaus Riggenbach's visit of 1868 to inspect the Mount Washington line.

4

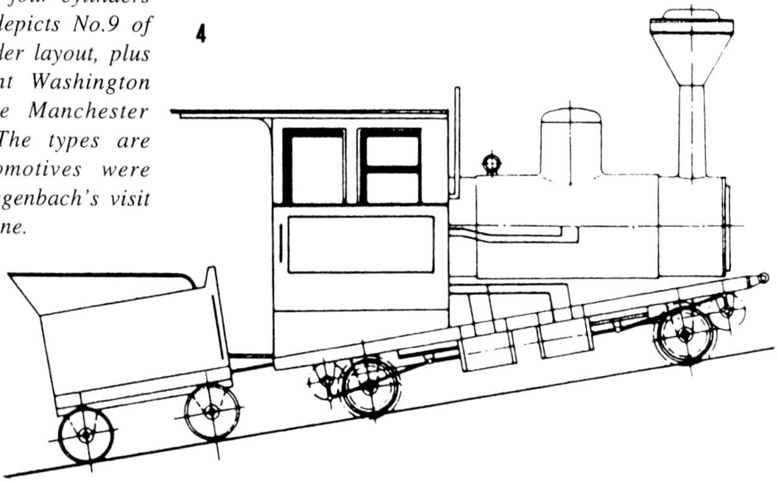

1869 and was about 3 miles long with an average gradient of 1 in 4 and a maximum of 1 in 3. Known as a 'cog wheel' railway, Marsh used a ladder type of rack with circular rungs fixed securely between the running rails. The teeth of a vertical pinion wheel under the locomotive meshed with the spacers between the ladder rungs.

An interesting feature was that the line was laid on timbers on the ground, some becoming trestles as the track crossed depressions in the ground. "Jacob's Ladder" is the best known of these trestles. The Mount Washington Cog Railway was built to the narrow gauge of 4ft 7in. Even though only 1½in narrow by todays standards, it was indeed narrower than when 5ft 0in, 5ft 6in and 6ft 0in were in use on that Continent. Built as a passenger carrying line to transport holiday makers to the summit the little 7 ton locomotive required one hour to make the climb, pushing ahead of it a passenger car weighing 4 tons. The first locomotive was known as *Peppersass* because her vertical boiler topped by a large balloon stack reminded people of a bottle of a popular luncheon condiment of the time. The Mount Washington Cog Railway(as it is known today)currently advertises itself as "An unforgettable journey to the top of New England" and operates up to 8 locomotives at any one time with hourly departures of one or more trains from early morning to late afternoon during the Summer season.

In Europe a Fell system centre-rail railway(without rack)opened in June 1868 between St.Michel due Maurienne, in France, and Susa, in Italy, over the Col du Mont Cenis climbing to 6860ft above sea level. This was to survive only 3 years or so until the opening of the Mont Cenis tunnel in 1871.

Owing to the rapid and enormous development of the railways, many improvements were made in locomotive construction, and great progress was attained. The necessity of dealing with heavy trains on lines with very steep gradients naturally called for heavy locomotives with an increased number of coupled wheels. This required special designs and led to the adoption of axles with lateral play, plus a large number of articulated and semi-articulated locomotive designs.

The mountainous nature of the country in Switzerland gave particular opportunity for designing special locomotives. In normal adhesion railways a gradient was permissible up to 1 in 40(the Gotthard Railway), and in secondary railways as much as 1 in 20(South Eastern Railway). The Uetli Mountain Railway formed an exception as it had gradients of 1 in 15 and the purely adhesion locomotive used on this line could when developing its utmost power, draw a train after it of a weight equal to itself.

Experience has shown that for mountain railways the limit for adhesion was a maximum of 1 in 25, but it was better not to go higher than 1 in 28½ and that if the

The colour card from which this photograph is reproduced was posted in 1906 and shows Jacobs Ladder, on the Mount Washington Railway. The locomotive was built as the second No.4 "Atlas", in 1875 by the Manchester Locomotive Works and was damaged in an 1895 fire, rebuilt and renumbered '2' becoming the fourth locomotive to carry this number. Its name was "Ammonoosuc". At the lower end is a four-wheel baggage trailer. The date circa 1895-1900. *C.J.Walker collection*

No.8 "Tip Top" was originally named "Pilgrim" and was built by the Manchester Locomotive Works in 1892. It was photographed on a colour card published by Chisholm Bros., Portland, ME, and produced in Germany. Although undated the cost of postage was "one cent United States and Island Possessions, Cuba , Canada and Mexico. Two cents for Foreign". *C.J.Walker collection*

Base station, Mount Washington Railway, White Mountains, New Hampshire. From a 1906 postcard by Detroit Publishing Company. *C.J.Walker collection*

railway had steeper gradients than this, rack-gear should be used. In actual fact the steepest Swiss gradient operated by adhesion is 1 in 13¾.

For railways on the mixed system of driving by adhesion and by rack-gear, 1 in 8½ gradients should not be exceeded in order to obtain economical working of the system.

On purely rack-railways gearing vertically into the rack (Riggenbach, Abt and Strub systems), it was recommended that the maximum gradient should not exceed 1 in 4. By careful design of the road and with the rack maintained in good condition, combined with the use of suitably designed locomotives, safe working was ensured both when trains ascend or descend. For gradients up to 1 in 3.3 it was necessary to be most accurate in the control of the rack-teeth, as when the train is braked going down banks, very small differences assist the rack-wheel to mount on the rack.

If the contour of the country required a still steeper gradient, it was necessary to use a rack with lateral gearing(Locher's system).

NIKLAUS RIGGENBACH AND THE RIGI RACK RAILWAYS

Niklaus Riggenbach was for 20 years(from 1853) Locomotive Superintendent of the Central Railway of Switzerland in Olten and he had had much to do with the introduction of railways to that country. Part of the C.R. of S., passed beneath the Hanenstein, between Basle and Olten. On this section was a steep climb from Sissach and extending about 6 miles with a gradient of 1 in 47½ to Laüfelfingen, where the main tunnel began.At the tunnel entrance the rising grade increased to 1 in 38½ and continued to Olten station. The length of this steeper section was about 5½ miles of which 1½ miles lay within the tunnel. Riggenbach found that his conventional 0-6-0 locomotives could take 120 tons up the 1 in 38½ in the open, but could only manage 90 tons through the tunnel due to wet and slippery rails. This state of affairs resulted in a reduction of 25% in the effective work done by the locomotives and Riggenbach began to think of ways of overcoming these problems, eventually coming to the conclusion that a rack-rail would be the best solution. On 12 August 1863 after trying various models, Riggenbach patented an improved method of constructing rack-rails and locomotives having toothed gear-wheels meshing with the rack. The French patent was taken up by the locomotive building firm of André Koechlin et Cie(Mulhouse).

Following this, Riggenbach set about trying to find a suitable location on which to build a steep gradient railway employing his rack system, but it was not until 1869 that the opportunity arose. In 1868 Riggenbach had journeyed to America to inspect the Mount Washington Railway and on his return to Switzerland in the following year, set about construction of a 4ft 8½ gauge rack/adhesion line from the Swiss Central

Railway, running to quarries at Ostermundingen, near Bern. This experiment proved that Riggenbach's idea actually worked, and along with several associates he looked around Switzerland for a suitable location on which to make a large scale experiment using rack propulsion.

The chosen location was the Rigi, a mountain close to the Lake of Luzern. Riggenbach, along with his partners Naeff and Zschukke, set about obtaining a concession from the Canton of Luzern, construction commencing in November 1869. The 4ft 8½in gauge Rigi Railway commenced at Vitznau(on Lake Luzern)and proceeded up the mountain terminating originally at Staffelhöhe, ¼ mile short of and 650 feet below the summit, this section opening on 23 May 1871. On 23 December 1872 the Federal Railway Act came into being. This still allowed private railway construction but the Federal Government took over from the various Cantons the right to grant concessions for new construction. From this date all plans for new construction had to be submitted to Bern for approval. The reason why the Rigi Railway extended only from Vitznau to Staffelhöhe was that this was the frontier between the Cantons of Luzern and Schwyz and at that time there was considerable rivalry between the two. Since the Rigi was started before the Federal Railway Act came into being, the Canton of Schwyz was in order to refuse the Rigi Railway permission to cross its borders. There was of course an ulterior motive since the Schwyz Canton realised the tourist potential and determined to build its own railway to the summit. Accordingly a group of citizens of Arth, a town at the southern end of the neighbouring Lake of Zug, obtained a concession from the Canton of Schwyz authorising construction of a new railway from the Gotthard Railway junction of Arth-Goldau, up the east side of the Rigi, to Staffelhöhe, and from there to the summit. Construction commenced on the upper section from Staffelhöhe, to the Kulm(summit station)and this was handed over to the Vitznau-Rigi Railway, the Arth Rigi Company receiving 60% of the gross receipts from the operation of this upper section which opened on 27 June 1873. The separate 6.1 mile long Arth-Rigi Railway from Arth Goldau opened on 4 June 1875 and had its own independent track to the summit so that today there are double tracks from Staffelhöhe to Rigi Kulm. The ARB was electrified on 20 May 1907. It has a ruling gradient of 1 in 5.

In the early years the Rigi had been opened by the two mountain railways and there were no fewer than 16 hotels on different parts of the main ridge offering somewhere in excess of 1800 beds. At Kaltbad a 4 mile - 1 metre gauge branch ran along the crest of the ridge to Scheidegg, but this is no longer in existence and indeed many of the hotels are closed down also.

The following description of the Rigi Railway is extracted from *Engineering* for 29 March 1872: "The Rigi Railway starts at Vitznau, on the shore of the Lake Lucerne, and extends a distance of 5760yards, or about 3¼ miles, to the station at Staffelhöhe, a short distance above Rigi Kaltbad, the well-known hotel and establishment for cold baths .... the line rises 3937ft, the gradient being at first 1 in 14.9, while after getting clear of the town of Vitznau it varies from 1 in 5.56 to as steep as 1 in 4, the average gradient for the whole distance being 1 in 4.45. The curves are all of radius 590½ft .... The principal works on the lines are a tunnel 246ft in length and a bridge over the Schnurtobel, of three spans, and a total length of 279ft. Both the tunnel and the bridge are on a gradient of 1 in 4 .... The bridge is also on a curve. It consists of three spans of 83ft 8in each and is composed of two plate girders 3ft 11¼in deep, placed 6ft 10⅝in apart from centre to centre, and connected every 5ft by T irons and diagonal bars .... Longitudinal timber sleepers and footways are provided. The total width of the bridge between handrails is 13ft 9in. .... For a great part of the length of the line the bed for the cross-sleepers is formed by cutting away the rock its-self to the depth of about a foot. The cross-sleepers are 6in deep, 8in wide, and 7ft 10½in long and they are placed at a distance apart of 2ft 5½in from centre to centre. Upon them are spiked the carrying rails of Vignoles section, and weighing 35lb per yard, and also the central rack. Besides the rails there are also fixed to the cross-sleepers the longitudinal guard timber having a section of 6in by 7in. The carrying rails are laid to 4ft 8½in gauge and the whole permanent way is prevented from slipping down the steep gradient by the cross-sleepers being made at intervals of about 250ft, to take a firm abutment against masonry piers let into the solid rock.

The central rack into which the toothed wheels on the locomotives and carriages gear, is formed of two channel irons, each 4¾in deep, by 2⅝in thick. These two channel irons are placed 5in apart, and into them are rivetted the ends of a series of pins or teeth formed of wrought iron. These bars or teeth are placed at a pitch of 3.94in and they are 1.42in deep, by 1.42in wide on the upper, and 2.16in wide on their lower sides. ..... At their ends where they are rivetted into the channel irons, they are rounded at their sides ... The central rack we have been describing is made in lengths of 3 metres(9ft 10in), these lengths being united by fish-plates bolted to the lower flanges of the channel irons. On the curves the teeth or bars are made to converge to the centre of an arc of 590½ft radius.

At each of the termini and at an intermediate point at the middle of the line, is placed an arrangement for shifting the trains from one line of rails to another. The employment of toothed wheels gearing into a central rack rendered ordinary switches inapplicable ... the arrangement used consists of a kind of part turntable, or rather swing bridge, turning on a pivot at one end, carrying a line of rails, which can be made to agree with either line of rails. The turntable is altogether 49ft 3in long and is supported at two intermediate points by wheels travelling on the rails. The table is shifted by gearing acting on a toothed rod connected to the table.

The locomotives used .... on the Rigi Railway .... constructed by M.Riggenbach, at the workshops of the Central Swiss Railway at Alten(Olten). ...The engine is carried on four wheels, the boiler being of the vertical type situated midway between the two axles. The boiler is so fixed to the frame, that its axis is vertical when the engine is standing on a gradient of 1 in 5.263. The wheelbase is 9ft 10in. The cylinders are 10⅝in diameter with 15¾in stroke, and they are fixed to the outside of the frames by the side of the boiler. The valve gear is of the straight link kind, and is actuated by eccentrics mounted on overhung cranks. ...The connecting rods are coupled to cranks on the end of a shaft carrying two pinions each of 8.67in diameter. These pinions have each 14 teeth and they gear into spur wheels, with 43 teeth, keyed on the driving or lower axle. On this axle are placed the lower carrying wheels while there is also keyed on its centre the toothed wheel which gears into the central rack. This wheel is 2ft 1in diameter and has 20 teeth. The second or upper axle is also provided, besides its carrying wheels, with a central spur wheel which gears into the central rack, this wheel being employed for arresting the motion of the trains by means of the brakes. For this purpose there are on the axle between the toothed wheel and the carrying wheels two pulleys, which can be clipped by hanging brake blocks which are brought into action by means of links and levers actuated by ordinary brake screws on the tender. The crank shaft also carries a brake pulley of small diameter ... its circumference having a number of V grooves turned in it so as to increase the grip of the brake blocks which are applied by the aid of the handwheel(nearest to the boiler).

... a retarding power is exerted by counter pressure in the cylinders during the time the train is descending. Thus when a descent is being made the steam is shut off from the cylinders by a handle(on the steam line mounted on boiler)and the pistons are allowed to pump air, this being drawn in through an opening in the box connected with the exhaust pipe and being forced into the steam pipe, whence it escapes through a cock provided. The box contains two valves, one covering an opening in the bottom communicating with the external air, while the other closes the communication with the upper part of the exhaust pipe, this portion of the pipe being bell-mounted at its lower end to afford space for the valve to work. Both these valves open by being lifted, and their spindles, are connected by a lever vibrating on an intermediate fulcrum, the arrangement being such that when one valve is opened the other is necessarily closed. When the exhaust steam is admitted to the box, the pressure opens the valve leading to the upper part of the exhaust pipe, and closes that communicating with the external air, while, when the cylinders are drawing air from the box, the exhaustion opens the valve communicating with the external air, and closes that communicating with the upper part of the exhaust pipe, thus preventing dust and ashes from being drawn into the cylinders from the smokebox. Also whilst the descent is taking place, a small stream of water from the tender is turned into each cylinder to prevent the latter from working dry, and by adjusting the opening of the escape cock, the counter pressure of air against the pistons can be regulated to any desired amount.

To prevent any chance of derailment in the case of the spur wheels getting out of gear, there are, at each end of the engine, strong guard irons curved inwards at their lower ends. ...At its lower end the engine carries a tank

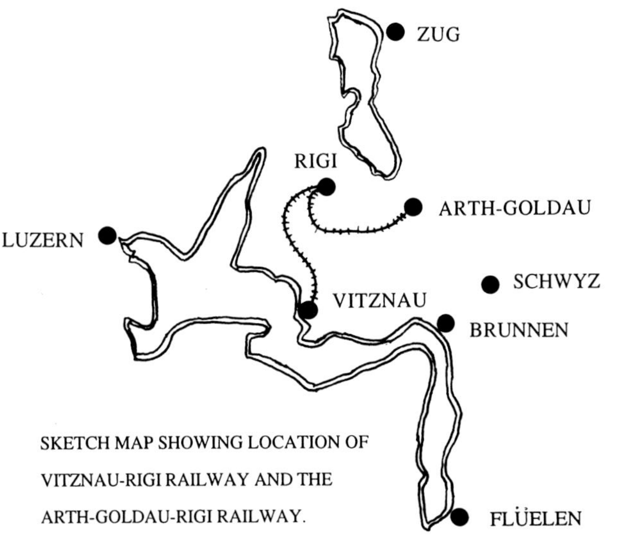

SKETCH MAP SHOWING LOCATION OF VITZNAU-RIGI RAILWAY AND THE ARTH-GOLDAU-RIGI RAILWAY.

Not to Scale
© D.Binns

and fuel bunker, ... at the upper end there is a receptacle for passengers luggage, this receptacle having open trellis sides. The weight of the engine in working order is 12½ tons.

The train consists, besides the locomotive, of a single passenger carriage having open sides. The weight of the vehicle is 4 tons and it carries 54 passengers on nine seats, six on each. The seats all face down hill. This vehicle is carried on four wheels, each of the two axles being provided besides the carrying wheels, with two brake pulleys and a toothed wheel, gearing into the central rack. The carriage ... is not coupled to the engine but the headstock at the lower end merely abuts against a buffer on the engine."

As we have noted above the first six Vitznau - Rigi Railway locomotives were built at the Swiss Central Railway shops at Olten. These were constructed with vertical boilers, as under:-

No.	Name	Olten Works' No's	Year
1	*Stadt Luzern*	17	1870
2	*Stadt Basel*	18	1871
3	*Stadt Bern*	19	1871
4	-	21	1872
5	-	22	1872
6	-	23	1873

These were rebuilt with horizontal boilers at Olten:-

No.	Rebuilt Year
1	1882
2	1883
3	1884
4	1886
5	1886
6	1891

Later locomotives - No's 7-10 of the VRB were built to Riggenbach's plans by the Schweizerischen Lokomotiv und Maschinenfabrik(SLM), at Winterthur. These carried SLM Works No's 1-4/1873.

The following is extracted from a paper by Mr T.Weber, Managing Director, and Mr S.Abt, Works Engineer, of SLM, Winterthur, which was read at the July 1911 Zurich meeting of The Institute of Mechanical Engineers entitled *"Rack Railway Locomotives of the Swiss Mountain Railways"*.

"(a) Locomotives with Rack-Gear only. As already stated, in May 1871, the now well-known Vitznau-Rigi Railway was opened as the first European rack-railway for passenger traffic. The gauge is the ordinary English gauge. The line has a length of 4.38 miles and gradients from 6 per cent. up to 25 per cent., the mean gradient being 20 per cent. The curves have 591ft radius. The original road was built with longitudinal and cross-sleepers, but between 1885 and 1895 the road was rebuilt, the timber sleepers being replaced by iron ones, and the iron rails being replaced by steel rails.

The first locomotive for this line was built in the works of the Central Railway in Olten; the engine had a vertical boiler similar to the engines on Mount Washington in order to reduce as much as possible the variations in water-level arising from the different gradients over which the engines worked. Following locomotives were built by SLM in Winterthur, and were the first work turned out by that firm. After eleven years use the vertical boilers were replaced by horizontal ones.

The appended diagram shows the vertical boiler engine carried on two axles, on the lower of which is mounted running loose the driving cog-wheel which is driven by gearing from the crankshaft. The cylinders lie on both sides outside the frames, and drive the intermediate shaft by means of connecting-rods and cranks. The upper axle carries a toothed brake-wheel with an arrangement to be used in case of an accident to the driving wheel. The ordinary brake works on the discs of the crankshaft.

When going down hill, an air counter-pressure brake is made use of, that is, the valve-gear is reversed and the regulator is shut off. The pistons then draw air into the cylinder which is compressed up as far as the regulator. This braking is governed by throttling the exhaust of the compressed air by means of a valve worked by the driver.

In the latest locomotives of the Rigi Railway which were built at the Winterthur Works between 1899 and 1902, the cylinders are placed farther toward the leading end. The driving cog-wheel, which is driven by means of gearing from the intermediate axle, has a larger diameter and is placed close behind the front carrying-axle; the trailing carrying-axle is provided with rack-brake. The brakes are arranged in the same manner as on the old engines, but in addition a centrifugal governor is made use of, which automatically controls the maximum speed, at which point a steam-brake is put into action. This automatic speed-regulator(a special construction of the Winterthur Works)has to be applied, by order of the Swiss Railway Department, on all rack-locomotives in service of Swiss lines. The speed of the Rigi locomotives is 6.8feet per second(4.7 miles per hour), and the total weight of the train is between 25 to 28 tons, about 200 h.p., being developed by the engine".

The Vitznau-Rigi Bahn of today is of course a totally modern business with the introduction of electrification on 3 October 1937. It is now operated on 15 Kv/50Hz a.c. supply and has an operational length of 7498yards. Double-line operates from Freibergen to Rigi Kaltbad for a length of 2060yards. There is one tunnel(Schwanden)219ft long and seven bridges of 318ft total length. Station altitudes are :- Vitznau 1440ft above sea-level, Rigi Kaltbad 4767 ft and Rigi Kulm 5748ft. Present travelling time 35 minutes with electric traction vehicles running uphill at 11.2mph and 7.5mph downhill. The VRB is more convenient for passengers from the Luzern direction whereas the ARB caters more for people from the Zurich area.

According to "Engineering" for 5 May 1871 there were to be double-decked carriages seating 46 downstairs and 36 on top. Whether these ever entered service, or whether the design was abandoned in favour of single-deck 4-wheelers is not known. The interior of the double-deck coaches was reached by end doors whilst the upper deck was reached by a light iron staircase at one end only. At both ends of the carriage was a screw brake comprising toothed wheels engaging with the centre rack.

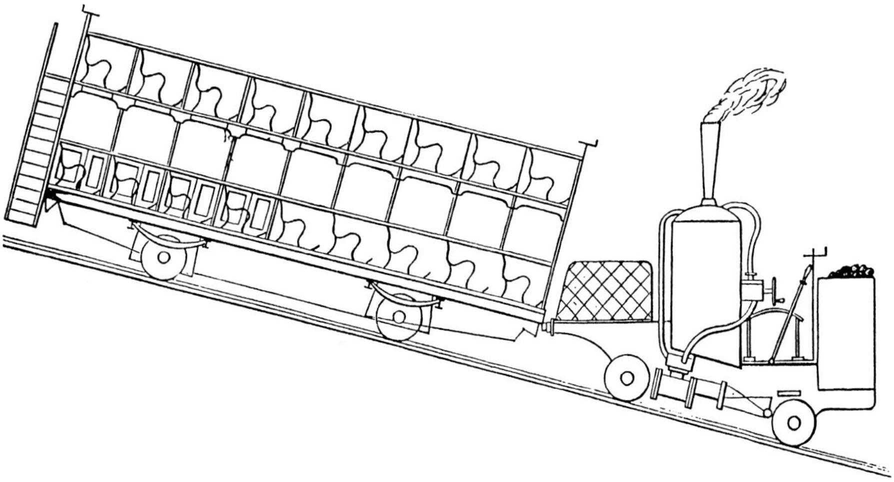

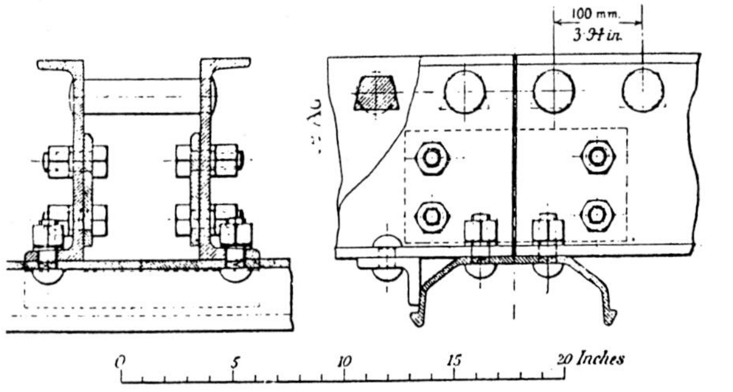

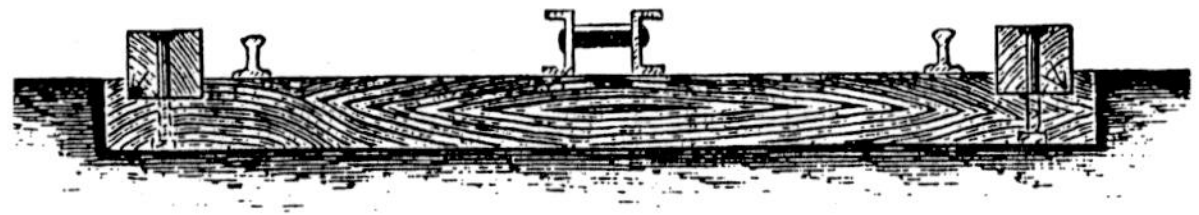

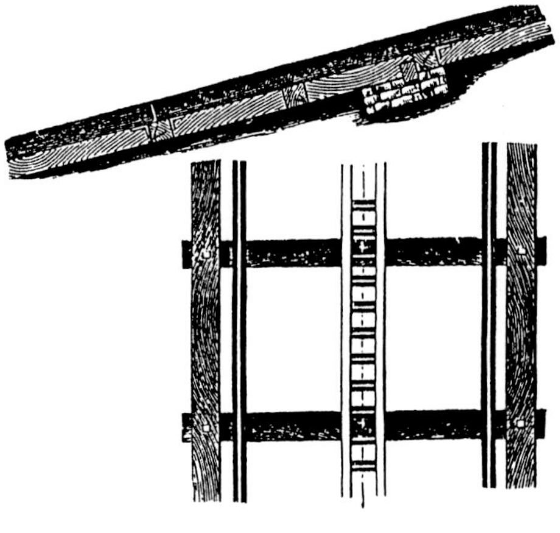

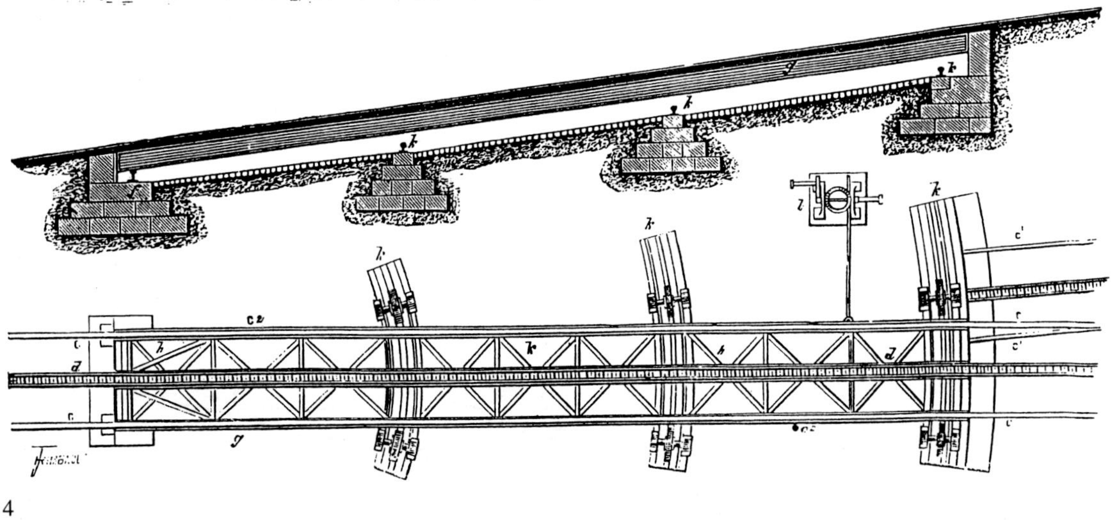

The original type of Vitznau-Rigi Railway vertical boiler rack locomotive is illustrated on this page. The vertical boiler was pressed to 135lb/sq in., and was so built that it assumed a vertical position when standing on a 1 in 5¼ grade. Water and coal supplies were located at the front end and at the rear was a space for luggage. The total wheelbase was 9ft 10in.

The 4-wheel carriage weighed 4 tons and carried 54 passengers on 9 seats, six on each, all facing downhill. This drawing shows the braking arrangement, each coach being fitted with two brake pulleys and a gear wheel operating on the centre rack. The brakes on each axle worked independently and were controlled from the end of the coach.

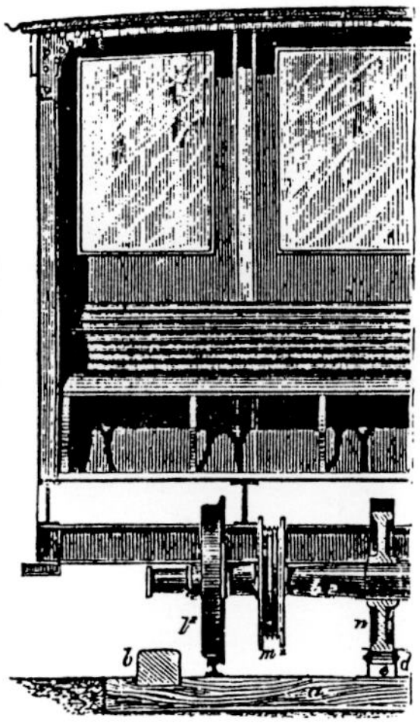

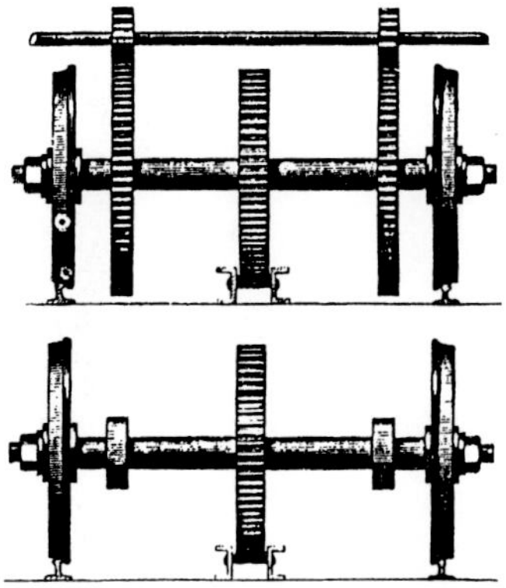

Opposite page: The use of gear wheels meshing with a central rack made ordinary point-work impossible so a sector plate was used. Its length of 49ft 3in was sufficient to hold both locomotive and single carriage, forming a complete train. The sector plate was supported at two intermediate places by wheels travelling on rails. Movement was achieved by gearing acting on a toothed rod, connected to the sector plate, and by these means trains were moved to a side track to allow other trains to pass.

Above: An early photograph on the Vitznau-Rigi Railway showing a single coach train pushed by an SLM four-wheeled locomotive from the series numbered 7-10.
D.Binns collection

Below: Diagram of series 7-10 built by SLM, Winterthur. D.Binns collection

Above No.10 as built by SLM, Winterthur. Works No.4/1873. SLM, Winterthur

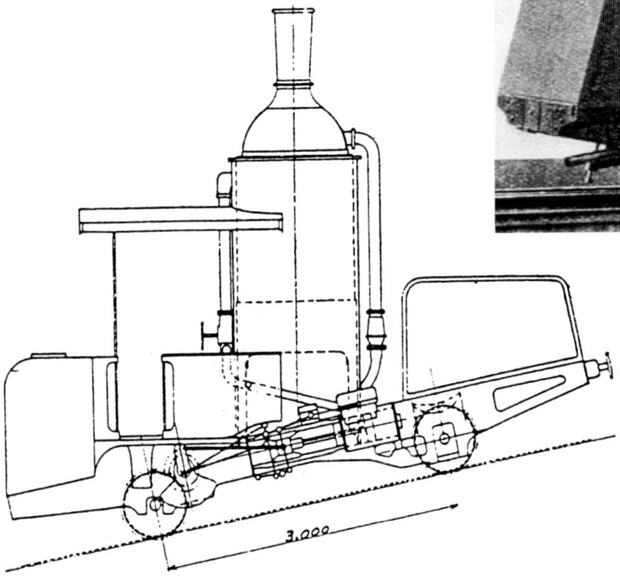

Built with vertical boiler				Rebuilt with horizontal boiler	
No.	**Builder**	**Works No.**	**Year**	**Year**	**Place**
7	SLM	1	1873	1892	SLM
8	SLM	2	1873	1892	SLM
9	SLM	3	1873	1891	Olten
10	SLM	4	1873	1888	Olten

No.9 as rebuilt in 1891 at Olten with a horizontal boiler. D.Binns collection

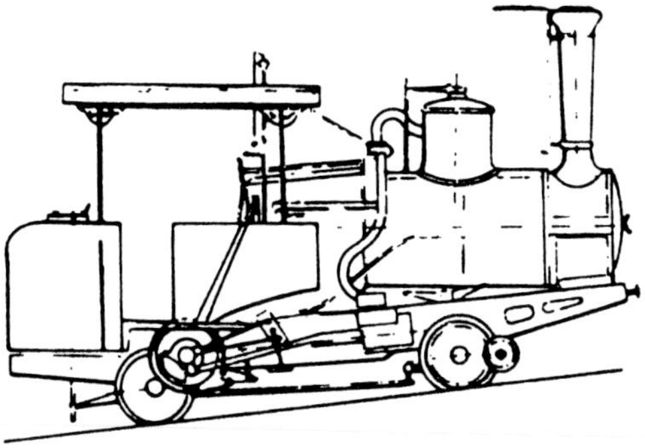

Drawing of No's 1-10 as rebuilt with horizontal boilers.

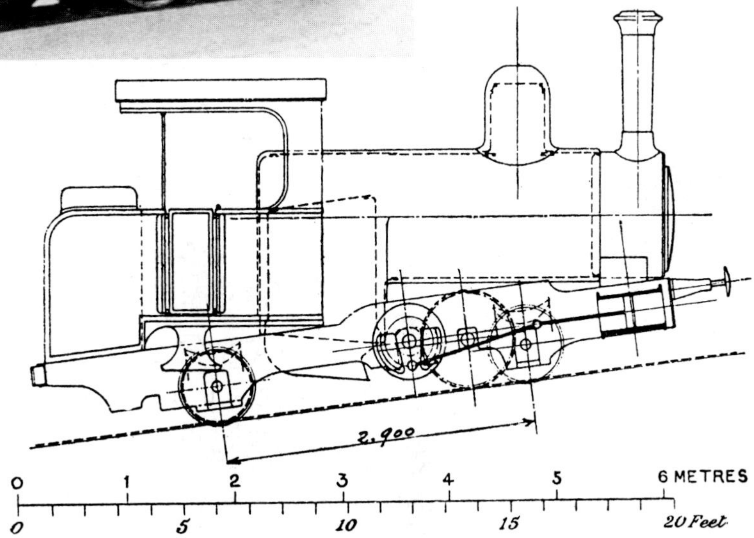

Above and right: VRB No's 11 and 12 were built in 1899 and 1902, SLM Works No's 1210/1899 and 1415/1902 and were the first new locomotives for the Vitznau Rigi Bahn built with conventional horizontal boilers. Previous to the arrival of the new pair, services had been maintained by No's 1-10 which originally had vertical boilers, but which were rebuilt with horizontal boilers from 1882. SLM, Winterthur

There was no No.13 on the Vitznau-Rigi Bahn. No.14 illustrated above was built at Aarau in 1875 and came into VRB stock in 1917.

Above and left: No.15(SLM Works No.2352)was added in 1913, followed by No's 16 and 17 of the same type, in 1923 and 1925.
SLM, Winterthur

On the Rigibahn. A train crosses the Schnurtobelbrüke on a steel girder bridge whilst Mount Pilatus stands majestically in the background.
P.J.Kelley collection

The Rigibahn station at Vitznau circa 1900 - from a colour card postmarked 1905. The locomotive is a rebuilt vertical boiler unit.
C.J.Walker collection

Preserved No.17 was seen on the VRB in recent years pushing a coach filled with happy school-children.
Marketing Rigibahnen

Rebuilt with a horizontal boiler No.10 was photographed at Rigi-Kulm. Undated photograph but probably around the turn of the century.
C.J.Walker collection

Railcar Bhe 2/4 No.3, built 1937, was observed with a trailer coach at Rigi Staffel on the Vitznau Rigi Bahn in June 1956. The Arth Goldau line is on the right. Voltage of both lines is 1500v dc.
P.J.Kelley

No.5 rebuilt from a vertical boiler locomotive, was photographed at Rigi-Kulm probably about the turn of the century.
D.Binns collection

The first five locomotives supplied to the Arth-Rigibahn are illustrated by this drawing. They were built by the Maschinenfabrik der Internationalen Gesselschaft für Bergbahnen, in Aarau in 1875 and carried Works and ARB No's 1-5. D.Binns collection

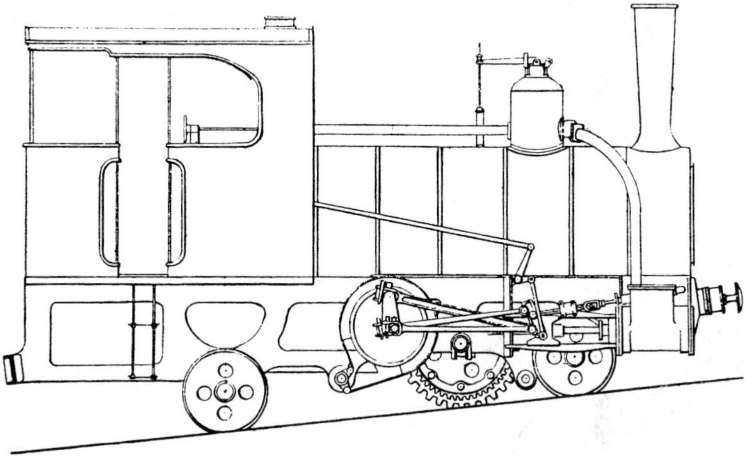

The engravings which follow are by J.Weber and reproduced from "The Arth-Rigi Railway" published by Orell Füssli & Co., Zürich, circa 1880. The engraving opposite depicts Rigi-Staffel.

Above: The Arth-Rigi Railway near Ober-Arth. Observe the conductor on look-out on top of the passenger car roof!.

Left: The Arth-Rigi Railway - Kräbelwand.

Below: An Arth-Rigi Railway train at Rothenfluh tunnel.

Bridge over the Rothenfluhbach. Arth-Rigi Railway.

Valley of Goldau with Arth-Rigi Railway train ascending.

Siding on the Arth-Rigi Railway showing the traverser employed to move trains from one track to another.

Arth-Rigi Bahn railcar No.13(SLM Works No.4121/1954)was photographed arriving at Rigi-Kulm on 11 June 1956. *P.J.Kelley*

The Rigi-Railway today with a modern 2-car shuttle train. In the background looms Mt.Pilatus and the Lake of Luzern.
Marketing Rigibahnen

RIGGENBACH - LOCOMOTIVE BUILDER

Following the initial success of the Rigi Railway and according to *Engineering* for 1 June 1877, Riggenbach had resigned from his post with the Central Railway of Switzerland in 1872 to devote himself to the construction of mountain railways. At that time(according to *Engineering*)he had no plans to establish a separate locomotive building firm and gave orders for rack-locomotives to SLM, Winterthur, on behalf of the Rigi Railway, or on account of the Société Internationale des Chemin de Fer de Montagne for locomotives for the following lines:- Rigi Railway, Kahlenberg Railway(Vienna); and the Schwabenberg Railway(Pesth). It was found that these locomotives were "not quite free from defects", and the Société

Internationale des Chemins de Fer de Montagne "thinking it advisable to retain the manufacture in their own hands decided to start their own workshops at Aarau, and from that time rack engines were built there under Riggenbach's superintendance". Thus Riggenbach and engineer Zschokke founded in 1873 in Aarau the 'Internationale Gesellschaft für Bergbahnen'. The first locomotives which were built in 1873 received Works No's 1-5 and were for the Arth Rigi Bahn. Works No's 6-8 were for the Rorschach-Heiden Bahn(on Lake Constance).The locomotive *"Elfe"* built in 1876 for the Materialbahn Ostermundingen-Steinbach - a line connecting quarries near Bern with the Swiss Central Railway, was allocated Works No.9. The latter locomotives were for use on mixed service rack/adhesion. Of other Aarau built locomotives little information appears to have survived, but may have included one for a line to the royal iron works of Wasseralfingen, Wurtemburg, and for the 4ft 8½in gauge line connecting the Swiss Union Railway at Rüti station with the works of M.Caspar Honnegger, over which ordinary railway wagons could be brought over 1 in 10 grades to the factory. The Rüti locomotive was in 1877 the smallest rack-rail locomotive made, weighing only 10 tons and capable of hauling a load of 25 tons up the 1 in 10.

The first three sketches illustrate locomotives built by SLM and ordered by Riggenbach starting with (1) Rigi Railway. (2) Kahlenberg Railway(Vienna), and (3) Schwabenberg Railway(Pesth).

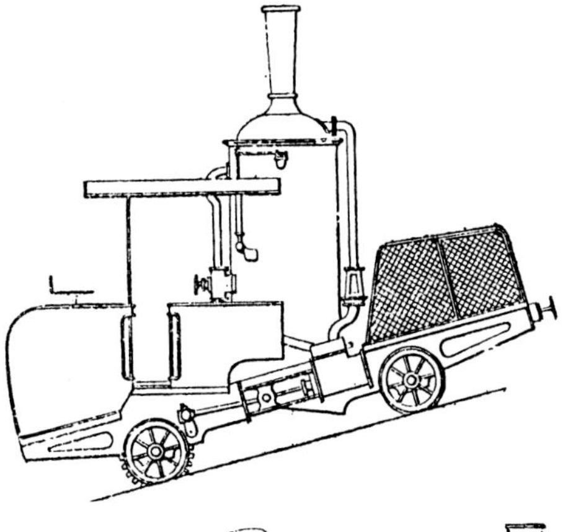

1

2

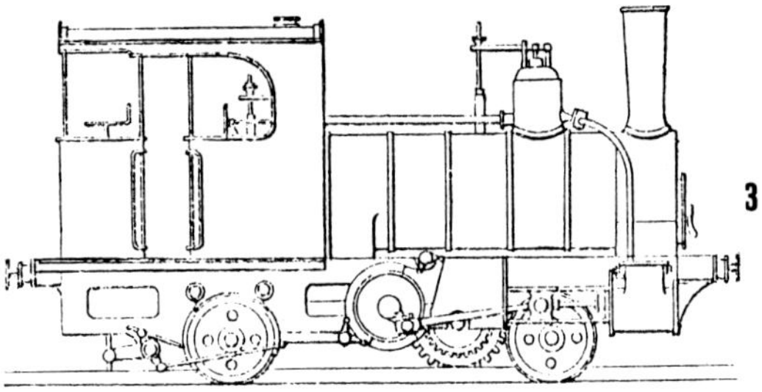

3

The next three drawings depict locomotives built by the Internationale Gesellschaft Für Bergbahnan in Aarau. (4) Arth Rigi Bahn. Works No's 1-5/1873, (5) Works No's 6-8/1875 Rorschach - Heiden Bahn. Road No's 1-3. (6) Works No.9(later 10)/1876 for the Materialbahn Ostermundingen-Steinbach. Road No.2 *Elfe.*

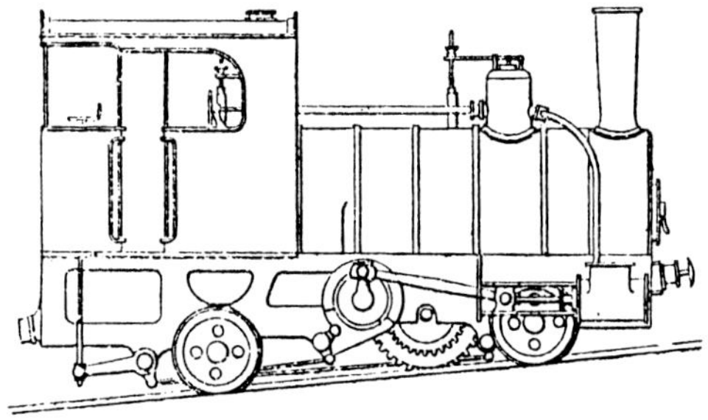

4

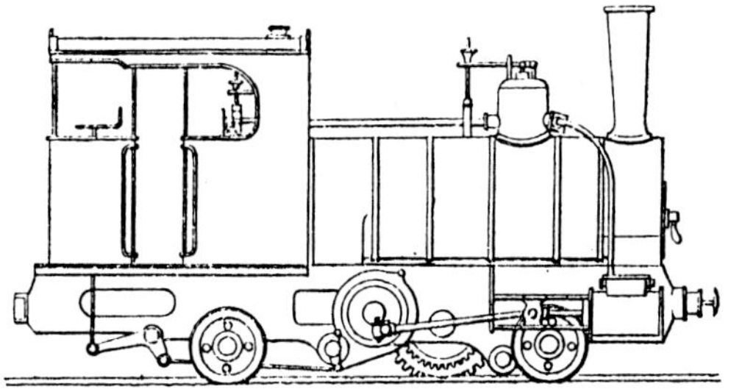

5

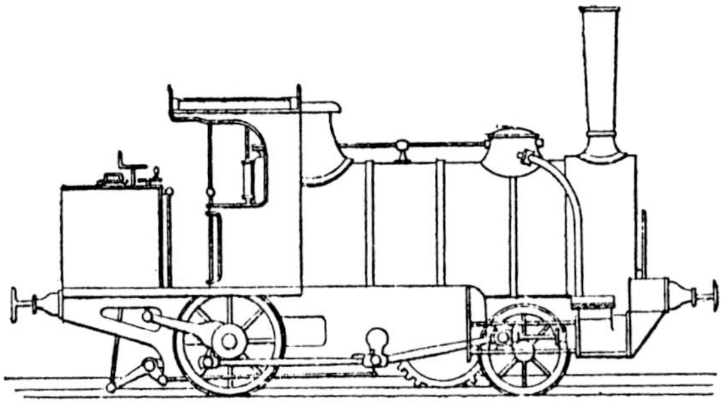

6

Drawing No.7 was No.1 of the Materialbahn Ostermundingen-Steinbach. Built by SCB at Olten in 1870, Works No.20 *Gnom.* (8) Represents a locomotive built to work on a line of the royal ironworks at Wasseralfingen, Wurtemburg(probably built at Aarau).

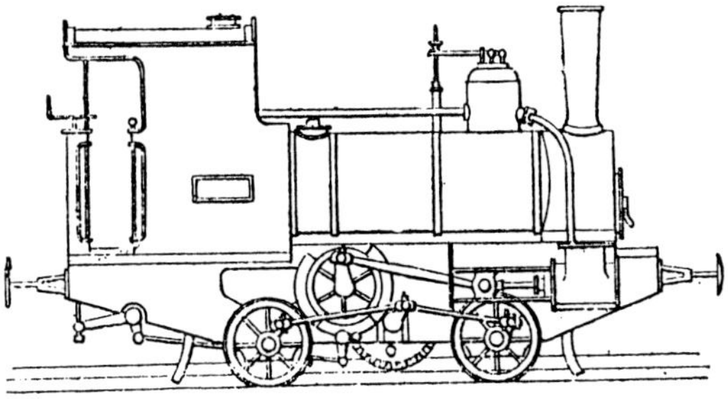

7

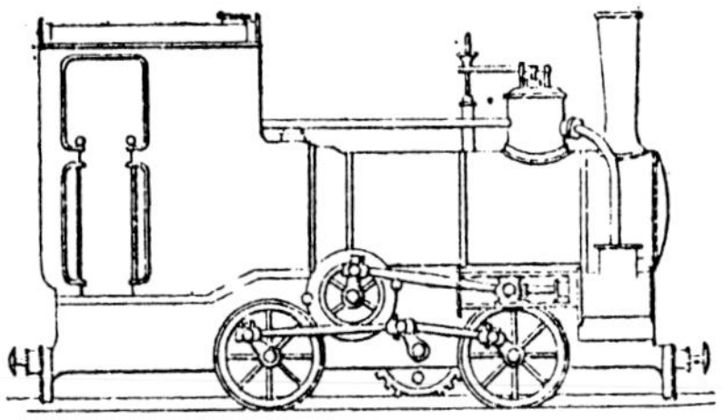

8

(9) Was the smallest rack locomotive built weighing 10 tons. For M.Caspar Honnegger, at Ruti(probably built at Aarau).

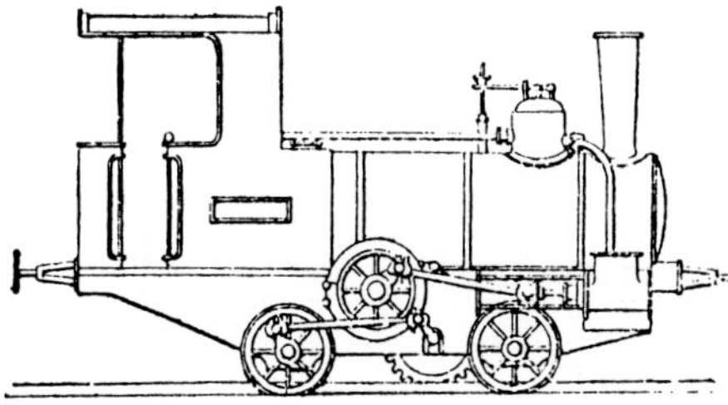

9

The reduction of orders and the economic crisis were the reason for discontinuing the firm in 1880. From this time on Riggenbach worked as a civil engineer in Olten until his death in 1899. Orders for cog-wheel locomotives were from 1880 to 1899 given to the engineering works at Esslingen, and also to the SLM, Winterthur.

Engineering for 1 June 1877 noted that there were then 32 of Riggenbach's rack-rack locomotives at work, these being as follows:-

Vitznau-Rigi	10
Kahlenberg(Austria)	6
Schwabenberg(Pest)	4
Arth-Rigi	5
Rorschack-Heiden	3
Ostermundingen	1
Ostermundingen	1
Wasseralfingen(Wurtemberg)	1
Rüti	1
	32

RACK TYPES

There are five types of Rack Systems in use in Switzerland.

1) The ladder rack of Niklaus Riggenbach(already described).

2) The double rack bar system of Dr Roman Abt. Although published, in 1884 it was not used until 1890, its first application being on the Mount Generoso Railway. The rack consisted of flat-toothed plates, of which two or three, according to the tractive power, were bolted together on chairs in such a way that the tooth of one plate in regard to the other was displaced of half or one-third of the pitch. This pitch amounts to 4.7inches. The Abt system of rack ensured a quiet motion of gearing, and allowed trains to work at higher speeds. It was specially applicable to long railways on the mixed system. The Abt rack is the most used of all the systems and circa 1911 about 323miles were fitted with it. In the earlier years of this century it was constructed by the Union Dortmünd, and by Cammell Laird and Co., of Sheffield.

3) The taper head rack bar of Emile Strub which used a broad-footed toothed rail having a wedge-formed top, similar to the rail used on rope railways, provided with clamp brake-gear. This head of the rack furnishes a good guide for the safety-grips; the latter, however, proved to be unsatisfactory when worked as brakes. Strub's rack-gear was first put into use in 1898 on the Jungfrau Railway. The pitch is generally 3.94 inches. The Bern foundry of L. v. Roll had taken over its construction.

4) The double gear-rack bar with horizontal gear wheels for ultra steep gradients, devised in 1886 by Colonel Edouard Locher for the Pilatus Railway. The wheels do not need any flanges because the centre rack rail holds the train in position. First used in 1888 on the Pilatus Railway, which has a maximum gradient of 1 in 2.08. The arrangement consisted of a plate having gear-teeth on each side of it, into which two gear-wheels drive, placed opposite to each other; these rack-plates, being riveted to a Vautrin rail, which is so rolled that guide-discs can be provided on the gear-wheel, ensure a correct guiding of the vehicle and prevent riding of the wheels. The pitch is 3.37inches. The heavy gradient necessitates a road very solidly built in masonry, the whole being properly anchored down.

5) A variation to the Riggenbach ladder rack was designed by Mr Klose(of semi-articulated locomotive fame)for the St.Gallen-Gais Railway.

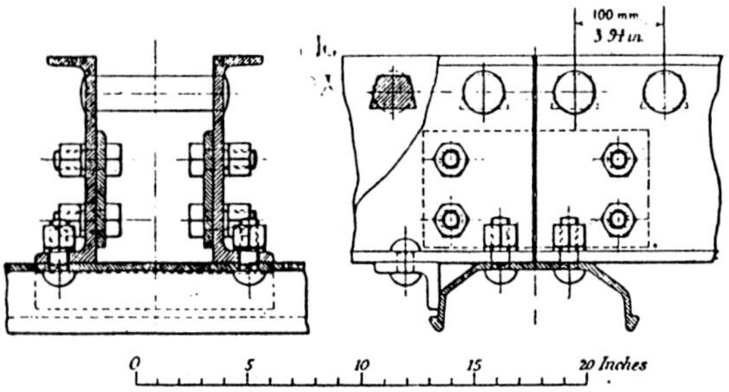

1

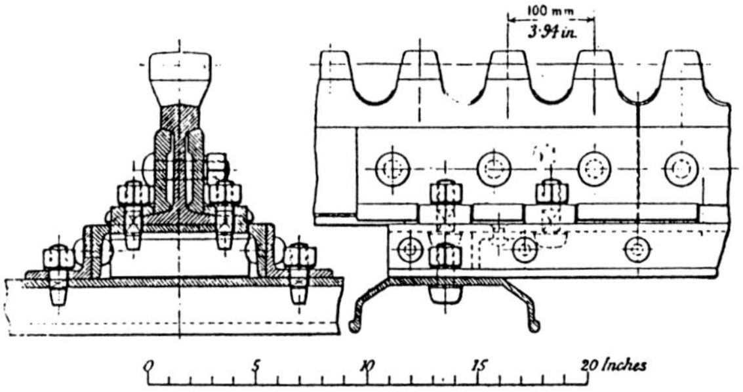

3

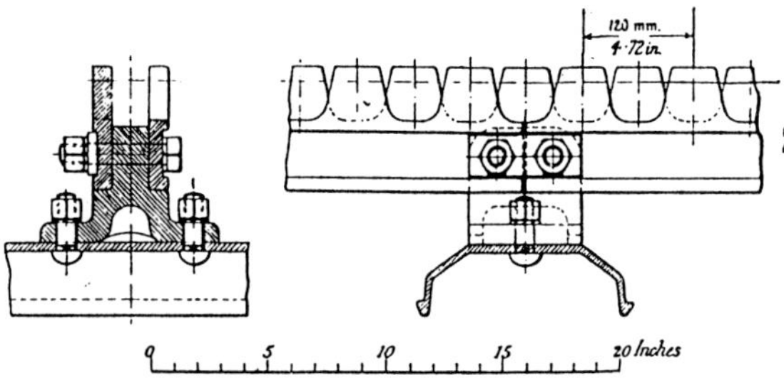

2

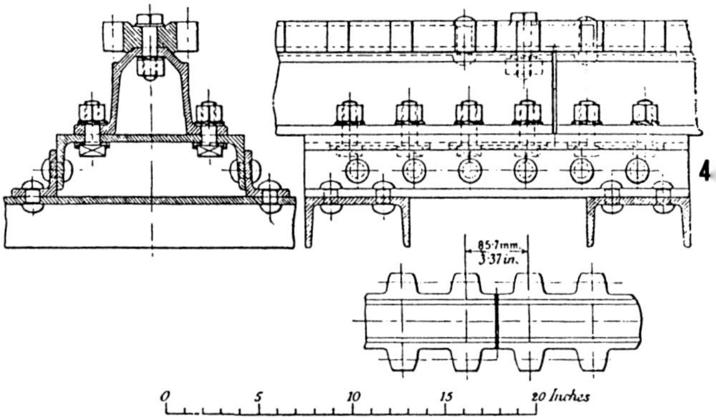

4

RIGI KALTBAD SCHEIDEGG BAHN

The 1 metre gauge Kaltbad Scheidegg Bahn diverged from the Vitznau Railway at Kaltbad and ran 4 miles along the crest of the ridge to Scheidegg. Opening on 14 July 1874 the line was steam worked throughout its existence, closing down in 1931 After official closure it was operated occasionally by an hotelier in 1933 and again at various times until 1942. All that now remains is the formation and trackbed.

The Scheideggstrasse(Berggasthaus Rigi-Scheidegg), now a footpath, but once the trackbed of the Rigi Kaltbad Scheidegg Bahn as it looked in 1954. *P.J.Kelley*

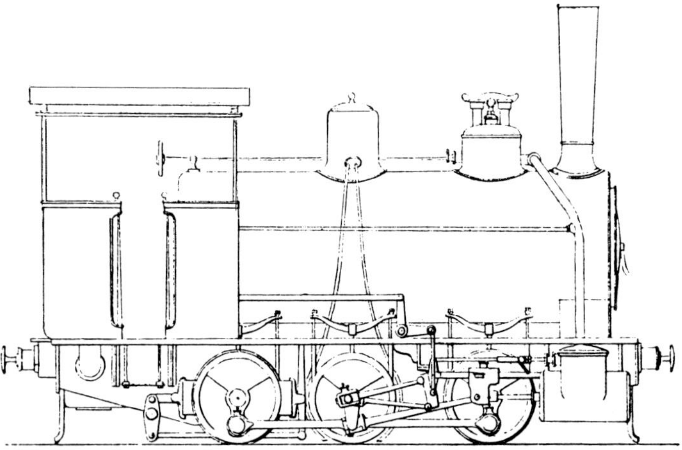

The Rigi-Scheidegg Bahn opened with three adhesion 0-6-0T built by SLM, Road No's 1-3, SLM Works No's 32, 34 and 37/1874. These were purchased at a cost of 35,000 Swiss Francs each locomotive. *D.Binns collection*

2

NARROW GAUGE MOUNTAIN RAILWAYS AROUND LUZERN

The following lines are covered in this chapter:-

	Type	Gauge	Opened	First Operated By	Date Electrified
Brünigbahn	R/A	1m	14 June1888	S	1941/2
Stansstad - Engelbergbahn (Luzern Stans - Engelbergbahn from December 1964)	R/A	1m	October1898	E	From Start
Pilatus Bahn	R	800mm	4 June 1889	S	15 May 1937
Brunnen Morschach Axenstein Bahn	R	1m	1 August 1905	E	From Start

SIMPLIFIED MAP SHOWING RAILWAYS DISCUSSED IN CHAPTER 2 i.e.,

BRÜNIGBAHN

STANSSTAD-ENGELBERGBAHN

PILATUS BAHN

BRUNNEN-MORSCHACH

AXENSTEIN BAHN

Not to Scale. © D.Binns

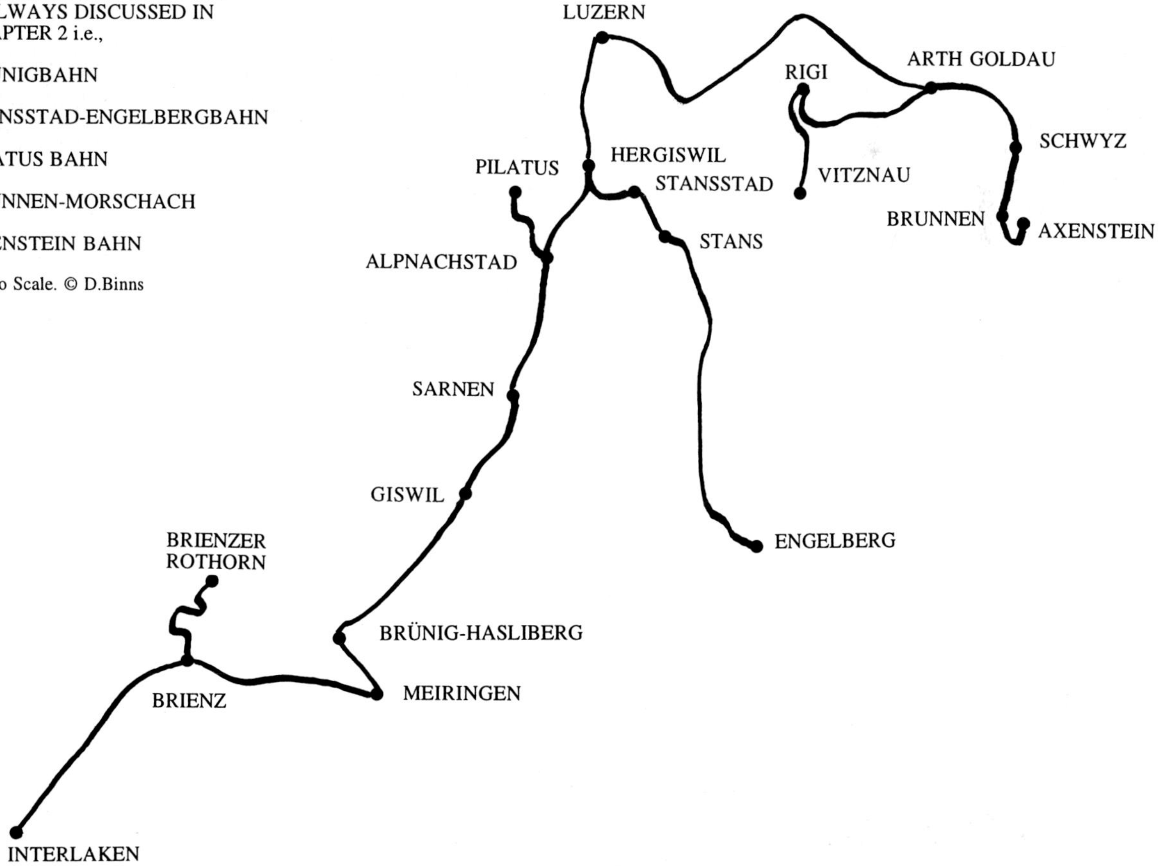

BRÜNIGBAHN

The 45.3 mile Brünigbahn links two popular areas of Switzerland, i.e., Luzern and Interlaken. This 1 metre gauge railway was originally to have been constructed to 4ft 8½in gauge following a concession granted in 1874 for a line from Brienz to Alpnachstad. Unfortunately finance could not be found and this was not forthcoming until a cheaper alternative was drawn up in the form of a 1 metre mixed rack/adhesion railway, construction of which started in 1886. Built by the Jura-Bern-Luzern-Bahn the section between Brienz and Alpnachstad opened in June 1888. At this stage the line was in isolation with no connections at either end to the main rail system. In 1889 the line was extended from Alpnachstad to Luzern and in the following year was absorbed by the Jura Simplon Railway, becoming part of the Swiss Federal Railways in 1903. After a considerable delay the line between Brienz and Interlaken opened in 1916. After much dispute over gauge it was decided to retain 1 metre and in 1941 the section between Luzern and Meiringen was electrified, with Meiringen to Interlaken in the following year.

The line is divided into three parts, that from Luzern to Giswil, and from Meiringen to Brienz and Interlaken being worked by adhesion, with the central section between Giswil and Meiringen incorporating four Riggenbach rack sections as the line crosses the Brünig Pass.

Today the Brünig route provides fast trains between Luzern and Interlaken as well as semi-fast and local services with some freight which is normally only conveyed on the adhesion sections.

A turn of the Century scene along the Brünig as a train poses for its picture on a rack section near the summit.
P.J.Kelley collection

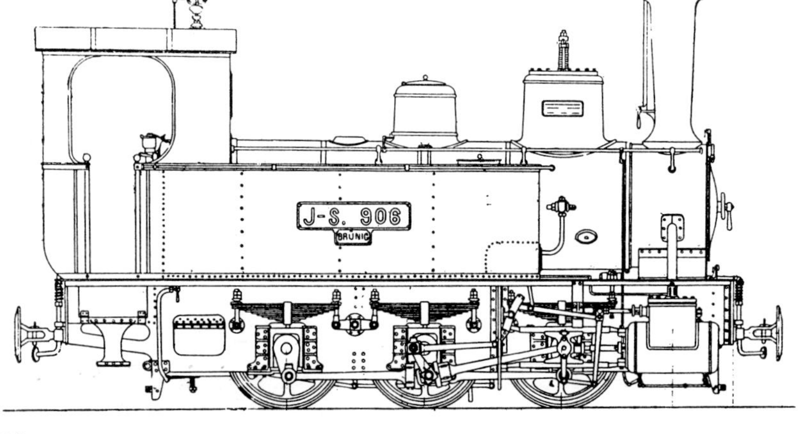

Ten of these 0-6-0T were built by SLM, Winterthur between 1887 and 1901 for use on the adhesion sections of the Brünigbahn. The first six(SLM 475/6 of 1887, 496-8/1888 and 584/1889)carried JBL No's 301-306, then JS 901-906 with 907-910(SLM 880/1889, 1089/1898 and 1341/2 of 1901)being added, the whole assuming SBB No's 101-110 in 1903. *D.Binns collection*

Brünig station at the summit of the Pass with rack locomotives and an abundance of rolling stock of varying designs and liveries. *P.J.Kelley collection*

The first rack/adhesion locomotives used on the Brünig Bahn are represented by this illustration of JBL No.352. These were capable of hauling 40 ton loads over 1 in 8½ grades at 6mph. Because the adhesion sections were short between the rack sections it was thought un-necessary to provide two sets of cylinders and gear, and in consequence the carrying wheels and the rack gear were coupled together and all worked by one pair of 13in x 18.9in cylinders. The Class was fitted with three different brakes:- A Rigi system(counter pressure brake)used when descending grades; a friction brake acting on the intermediate shaft; and a friction brake acting on a toothed wheel mounted loose on the leading axle, this wheel engaging with the rack. Klose automatic steam brake was fitted to the train. *"Engineer"*

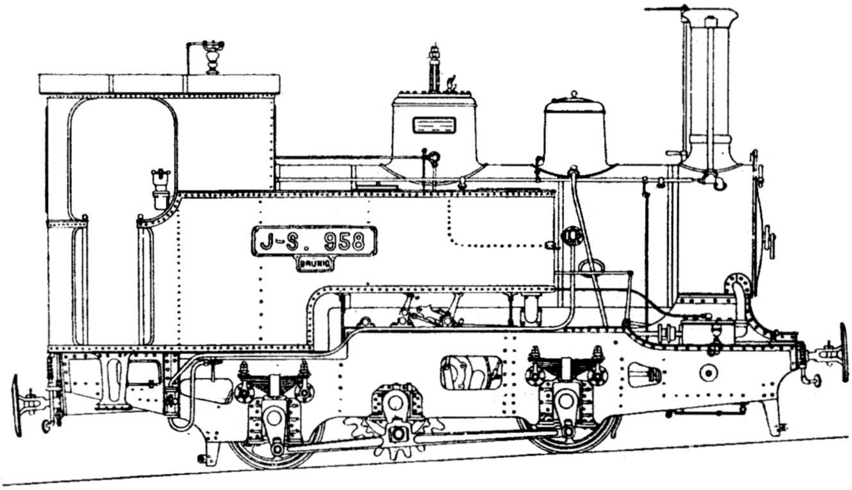

JBL 1887	JS 1890	SBB 1903	SLM No.	Built
351	951	1001	478	1887
352	952	1002	502	1888
353	953	1003	503	1888
354	954	1004	504	1888
355	955	1005	505	1888
356	956	1006	558	1889
357	957	1007	559	1889
358	958	1008	560	1889
-	959	1009	879	1894
-	960	1010	1192	1899
-	961	1011	1193	1899
-	962	1012	1339	1901
-	963	1013	1340	1901

An official photograph of No.1052, built in 1905.
SLM, Winterthur

SBB No's	SLM No's	Built
1051	1656	1905
1052	1657	1905
1053-5	1711-3	1906
1056/7	1831/2	1907
1058-61	1912-5	1908
1062-4	1992-4	1909
1065-7	2081-3	1910

An early view of the station at Brünig with a 1051 class engine heading a two-coach train.
P.J.Kelley collection

Rack/adhesion No.1053 at Meiringen on 8 July 1950. *Ian G.T.Duncan*

Eight larger 2-6-0T were supplied by SLM, Winterthur between 1906 and 1914 and these carried SBB No's 201-208. These were for use on adhesion sections of the line. 2-6-0T No.202 was photographed at Alpnachstad on the Brünig line in pre-electrification days. *D.Binns collection*

Works photograph of No.202 built in 1906.
D.Binns collection

Brünig No.	SLM No.	Built
201	1674	1906
202	1675	1906
203	2222	1912
204	2223	1912
205	2224	1912
206	2401	1914
207	2402	1914
208	2403	1914

2-6-0T No.206 was photographed at Meiringen on 9 July 1950. Ian G.T.Duncan

An undated view of the station at Alpnachstad and a train hauled by an unidentified 2-6-0T. *C.J.Walker collection*

Brünig Bahn Fhe 4/6 Gepack-Trieb wagen No's 908 and 912 at Meiringen on 9 July 1950. No.908 SLM Works No.3729/1941, 912 SLM Works No.3733/1941. *Ian G.T.Duncan*

The 09.21hrs train from Luzern to Interlaken at Hergiswil on 25 May 1954. Motor Luggage Van No.902. Built SLM 3723/ 1941. *P.J.Kelley*

The Brünigbahn links the Luzern and Interlaken areas and en-route crosses this bowstring girder bridge spanning the River Aare near Interlaken. Photographed on 26 May 1955. *P.J.Kelley*

STANSSTAD-ENGELBERGBAHN

The Stansstad Engelbergbahn was known by this title until 19 December 1964, when it became the Luzern Stans Engelbergbahn, a modernised metre gauge line running from Stansstad on the shores of Lake Luzern, to Engelberg, a climb of 1851ft in a distance of 14miles. It was a cross between a light railway and a tramway. A concession had been granted in 1890 for an electrified line from a jetty at Stansstad to Engelberg and by 1893 an electric tramway was in operation to Stans. The Stansstad-Engelberg-Bahn was formed in 1897 with construction of the remainder of the route being started. The line opened throughout in October 1898 and it was electrically operated on a 3-phase A.C.system of 850 volts at 32 cycles. The overhead line was of twin wires and the motor coaches had double bow collectors. Most of this 1 metre gauge line was adhesion worked but there was a Riggenbach rack section of 4920ft between Obermatt and Gharst. The gradient on the rack section was about 1 in 4 and as most of the railcars were not equipped for rack working, a 4-wheel locomotive was attached for this incline portion of the journey. The rack locomotives were also attached to the front of all motor coaches descending the rack to provide sufficient brake power. Gradients on the adhesion sections were up to 1 in 20.

In 1903 the tramway service from Stansstad jetty to Stans was withdrawn with the Stansstad-Engelberg-Bahn providing an alternative service. Amongst its activities the Company advertised "Train connection with the service of the Steamboat Co., at Stansstad. Connection with the Funicular Railway to Gerschnialp and the Air-Cable Railway to Trübsee(6000ft above sea level)".

The Depression of the 1930s resulted in a fall in tourist traffic and little investment was made. Indeed after World War Two the Company had insufficient resources to modernise but suffered also due to its isolation from the main rail system.

In 1956 the Confederation granted a concession to build a line from Stansstad to Hergiswil on the SBB Brünig line. The Company was soon placed in administration but construction of the Loppertunnel and the Acheregg bridge went ahead and soon there existed a physical connection between the local Company and the Brünig section of the SBB. At the same time, a major modernisation scheme was put in hand and on 19 December 1964 the existing Stansstad - Engelberg Railway became the Luzern-Stans-Engelberg Railway. The original railway had been rebuilt with new track to SBB metre gauge standards, new overhead electrification equipment at 15kv ac 16⅔ cycles and new rolling stock. Part of the original track bed was re-aligned. The railway had always been physically isolated having no connection with any other line. The Swiss Federal Railway station at Hergiswil was rebuilt to accommodate the Engelberg trains whilst the Engelberg Company provided new passenger and goods stations and a new repair depot at Stansstad. Existing train services were maintained during the period of improvement and modernisation. Five new 3-car trains composed of a 1080hp motor second, a centre coach(on four sets; on the fifth set the centre car is a luggage, parcels/post van)and a driving trailer composite. Mountain railway practice continued to apply on the 1 in 4 rack section where the motor coaches are always used at the lower end of the grade, pushing up the rack and leading on the descent. The new trains cover the 21 miles from Luzern to Engelberg in 1 hour.

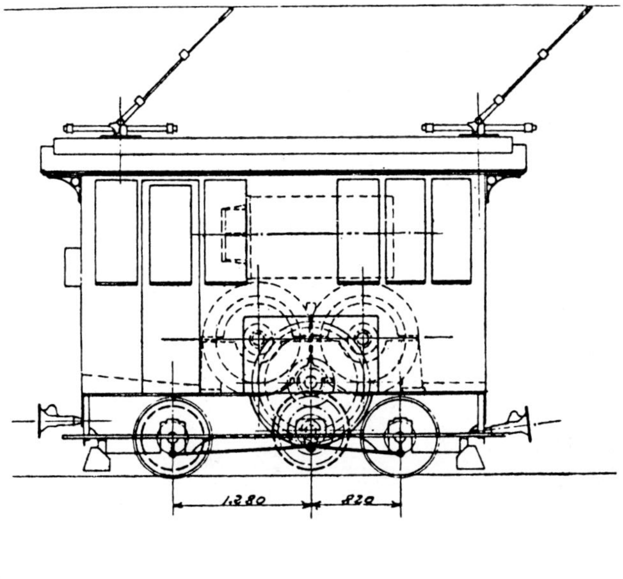

One of the electric rack locomotives used on the Stansstad-Engelberg Railway. Two motors developed 150hp each working by means of 'V' gearing and an intermediate shaft to the rack driving wheel. A special friction switch(designed by SLM)allowed the two carrying axles to engage as driving axles on adhesion sections by means of coupling rods. Speeds were 3.4mph and 7.1mph. Maximum tractive power 6.3 tons. D.Binns collection

Rack locomotive No.5 with trailer No.8, heads down hill in 1964. *Courtesy LSE*

Stansstad - Engelberg Bahn on 15 June 1956. Two rack locomotives in a siding at the depot between Obermatt and Grunenwald. The front one is HGe2/2 No.1 - SLM Works No.1139/1898. The second locomotive number is not known but was Works No.1666/1905. *P.J.Kelley*

At a point between Obermatt and Grunenwald rack locomotives are attached to the rear of trains for the rack section. The locomotive in the background is No.2(SLM Works No.1140/1898). This photograph was taken on 15 June 1956. *P.J.Kelley*

Rack locomotive No.2 in green and cream livery, dated back to 1898 and was photographed on 15 June 1956 waiting to set back after working a train up the rack section. *P.J.Kelley*

Railcar No.10 standing at Stansstad on 24 May 1954. This vehicle had probably been in use since the line opened. *P.J.Kelley*

The new Luzern Stans-Engelberg Bahn with a three-coach push/pull train headed by BDe 4/4 No.4 having just left Engelberg for Luzern. The motor coach is always at the downhill end as a safety measure due to the 1 in 4 rack gradient. *Courtesy LSE*

A push/pull train headed by composite driving trailer ABt No.28 fights its way through Winter snow en-route to Engelberg. *Courtesy LSE*

DRAHTSEILBAHN ENGELBERG GERSCHNIALP

The 1731ft long Drahtseilbahn Engelberg Gerschnialp was opened on 21 January 1913 with a height difference of 873ft . This metre gauge funicular climbed steeply at a gradient of 1 in 1½ hence the carriage compartments are stepped. The journey takes about 4 minutes and the last part of the trip is through a 90yard tunnel prior to reaching Gerschnialp. Each car takes 70 passengers. This funicular connects with Trübsee and the Jochpass.

Car No.1 descending on 26 May 1954. P.J.Kelley

Car No.2 descending on 26 May 1954. The platform is used for conveying luggage and skis. P.J.Kelley

DIETSCHIBERG FUNICULAR

A short distance from Luzern, in 1954 15 minutes on the trolleybus, one comes to Halde. Here is the lower terminus for the 1 metre gauge Dietschiberg Funicular. This line opened on 10 August 1912 and is 4125ft long. It has a total ascent of 610ft.

In addition to the glorious views at Dietschiberg there is an outdoor model railway based on the Gotthard and Lötschberg lines.

ARTH AM SEE - ARTH GOLDAU

This 1.6 mile tramway was built to 4ft 8½in gauge and ran from Arth Goldau to Arth am See. It opened on 4 June 1875 and was electrified 30 years later in 1905, closing on 31 August 1959.

Blue and white tramcar No.2 was photographed at Arth Goldau and unusually for Switzerland this had been built in Germany by Ver Maschfabrik Augsburg und Masch.Ges Nurnberg.Works No.63214/1905. P.J.Kelley

BRUNNEN-SCHWYZER STRASSENBAHNEN

The Brunnen-Schwyzer Strassenbahn was a metre gauge tramway from Schwyz to Brunnen, opening on 6 October 1900 with 4.4miles of line. Closure was effected on 15 December 1963 and it is believed the service was replaced by trolleybuses.

Tram No.5 of the Schwyzer Strassenbahnen was photographed at Brunnen Schiffstation on 13 June 1956. P.J.Kelley

THE PILATUS RAILWAY

One of the best known mountain railways in the Luzern area of Switzerland is that which climbs Mount Pilatus. This line is the steepest in the world worked by rack and pinion and with a maximum gradient of 1 in 2.08, required a special type of rack with teeth on both outer edges instead of on top. The track was of extremely solid construction, being carried on stone blocks fitted together. Opened on 4 June 1889 from Alpnachstad to Pilatuskulm the Pilatus Railway was first worked by steam, the 4670 yards required 70 minutes running to achieve the climb of 5344ft . It was electrified on 15 May 1937 on a 1550volts dc system when the journey time was reduced to 30 minutes up and 40 minutes down.

The success of the Rigi Railway prompted the Swiss engineers and financiers to investigate the possibility of a railway running up Mount Pilatus. None of the systems of steep railways then in use in Switzerland afforded any promise of being able to scale the sides of this gaunt limestone peak. During the mid-1880s surveys were made and it was found that by starting at Alpnachstad, a line was possible with an average gradient of 1 in 2.38, with a maximum of 1 in 2.08. A short model line was then made at this inclination and experiments were conducted using various different forms of rack with vertical teeth. The application for a licence to build the Pilatus Railway submitted by Edouard Locher in 1885 contained plans for a mono-rail railway, contrary to the ultimate version. The upper part of a 24in x 12in box-shaped steel girder was designed as a two-part rack-rail with slanting teeth. Small guide rails were fitted to the lower edges of the 'box' to act as a centring device. The individual 10 metre lengths of steel were to be joined by fishplates, each length supported by two iron braces. The locomotive would have had two symmetrically slanting tubular boilers - a completely new idea - between which the two cylinders, the connecting rod and the pinions lay. Of the two pairs of helical gears with inclined teeth, the front pair was linked to the connecting rod via two spur wheels and arranged as a spur gear. Broad grappling arms gripped under the sides of the 'box', thus preventing the locomotive from de-railing or mounting the teeth of the rack. It was seen that existing forms of rack construction were unsuitable for such severe grades, and when the engine was working hard the pinion was liable to mount the rack and therefor not safe. At this juncture, Colonel Edouard Locher suggested the use of two horizontal racks arranged back to back on a central rail, and gearing with two horizontal pinions, one at each side. This system was adopted for the Pilatus Railway, the rack rail being made in sections 3 metres long and for accuracy milled out of solid steel bars. Construction of the line had to be carefully considered. It was necessary to take precautions to prevent "creeping" of the rail downhill and at the same time ample allowance had to be made for contraction and expansion for the differences in temperature, which on Mount Pilatus could vary between 4° in winter and 104° in summer. The sleepers were bolted down with sling bolts which bound the masonry of the road bed and the iron superstructure into one solid mass.

The contract for the 800mm(2ft 7½in)gauge Pilatus Railway was awarded to Messrs Locher & Co., of Zurich, including rolling stock and stations. Design work was carried out by Messrs Locher, and Charles Brown, and by Weber, Hoffmann and Haas of SLM, Winterthur by whom construction of the rolling stock was undertaken. Work commenced after the spring thaw in 1886 with official trial runs of the new steam coach in the following Autumn. During 1888 a trial run was made to the summit, the train carrying journalists and technicians . Official examination of the Pilatus Railway(which had been built not a bit like the plans)was made and approval given on 17 May 1889 and the railway went into operation without any opening ceremony on 4 June following, opening for public service during the season May - October. The Kulm Hotel on Pilatus opened in 1890. The locomotives/cars were combined on the same underframe with the idea of saving weight(which would have been increased if they had been seperate). Several inconveniences resulted from this arrangement, but the saving in weight was of paramount importance. The combined locomotive carriage units were built by SLM. It was found that eight locomotives were insufficient to cope with the influx of passengers, so the steam coach which was the Swiss industry's showpiece at the World Fair in Paris, was quickly purchased. This arrived at Alpnachstad on 31 December 1889.

In order to reduce the resistance as much as possible the running wheels were flangeless, the unit being guided laterally by flanges on the central driving pinions which embraced the central channel iron forming the bed of the double rack rail, this reducing the friction particularly on curves, and also removing any tendency to mount or jump the rails. Careful consideration was given to the braking requirements of these combined locomotive/carriage units, the engine being fitted with (1) a brake on the crankshaft, worked by hand; (2) an air-brake with cooling arrangements as on the Rigi locomotives; (3) an automatic brake which came into

Hergiswil Church and Mount Pilatus on 25 May 1954.
P.J.Kelley

action when the descending speed reached 4.26ft per second. Frequently, Mount Pilatus was subjected to violent gusts of wind and as a further safety measure, the train was fitted with clips on each side embracing the rail heads - the clips being made long to prevent jamming, the connection with the carriage frame being such that a very slight amount of vertical play was allowed in the direction of the length. According to *Engineering* for 13 May 1887 "an engine is running daily from the lower station for conveying the materials of construction up the mountain; for this purpose the carriage part is removed and replaced by a platform". This unit is represented by the following diagrams. Note the cylinder position beneath the coal bunker at the lower end of the locomotive.

Engineering for 1 November 1889 details a locomotive /carriage for the Mount Pilatus Railway built by SLM, Winterthur and exhibited at the Paris Exhibition of that year. This was a modified version of the original with closed cab-back and closed passenger compartments. Mechanically the original and the modified versions were very similar, both being carried on two axles with flangeless wheels, the unit being guided entirely by the central rack. A paper read at the Zurich meeting of the Institution of Mechanical Engineers(entitled "*Rack Railway Locomotives of the Swiss Mountain Railways*")in July 1911 reported "The underframe of the coach forms at the same time a tender containing 800 litres(176 gallons)of water. The carriage is carried on two axles on three points. The boiler is of the ordinary locomotive form, but on account of the varying gradients it is placed transversely to the rails. The cylinders drive by a spur-wheel gearing on an intermediate axle, from which the power is transmitted by two pairs of conical wheels on the two vertical driving axles. At the lower end of these driving-axles the driving-wheels are placed together with their guide-rollers in order to ensure that the wheels gear properly into the rack. The leading gear-wheel is only used for the purpose of a brake, and its rollers have to guide the carriage against the Dantrin rail. The leading toothed-wheels run freely when the coach is going up the inclines, and they are locked when running down hill by means of a coupling through which they transmit reverse motion to two symmetrical worm-wheels, their axle carrying the brake-disc. By reason of the high gear-ratio, relatively small braking-power is sufficient to bring the train to a standstill. The brake is automatically put on when the speed-limit is exceeded. The following brakes are arranged: An air-compression brake when running down the banks, a frictional brake on the crankshaft, as well as friction and self-acting brakes on the leading pair of geared wheels as already described. The normal speed of the train is 4.72ft per second(2.7 miles per hour), the weight of the combined engine and carriage is 12 tons, and the engine develops 100 h.p. Very excellent results have been obtained by the use of superheated steam."

The original locomotive had its cylinders beneath the cab rear plate but on the modified version described above(and illustrated on page 48)they were located on the underframe beneath the front end of the carriage section.

According to *Engineering* for 1 November 1889 "All the materials employed for the construction of the trains are of a superior quality; the driving pinions are of crucible cast steel; the wormwheels are of Delta metal; they were carefully tested at the Ecole Polytechnique at Zurich by M.Tetmayer. The carriage is divided into four compartments, each accomodating eight passengers. The floors and seats are so arranged that they are practically level on the steepest incline. During the three years occupied in the construction of this line, which opened on 4 June last, the engines worked without any serious wear and tear. The line starts at Alpnach, at an elevation of 1434ft above the sea, and in the course of about three miles it rises to 6778ft, the time both of ascent and descent being about 1½ hrs."

The following dimensions are extracted from *Engineering* for 1 November 1889 and refer to the revised locomotives:-

Gauge 2ft 7½in
Cylinders 8.66in x 11.81in
Diameter of carrying wheels 15.75in

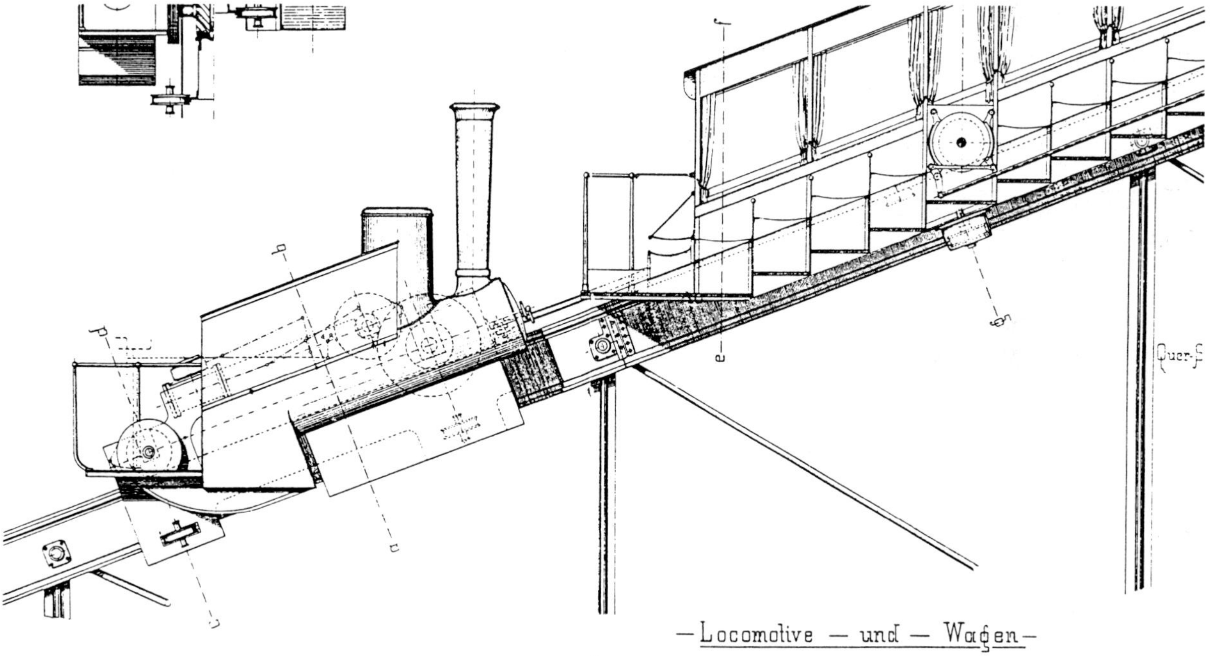

Locomotive and carriage for mono-rail as detailed in 1885 Pilatus Railway proposal. *D.Binns collection*

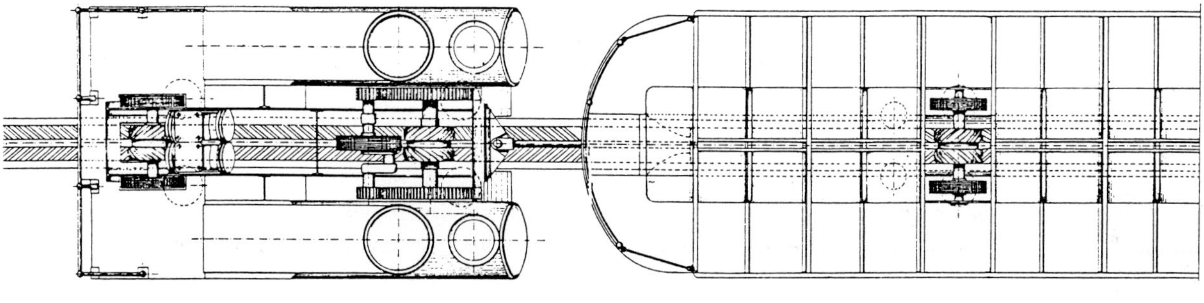

The Locher system of rack and pinion drive. The rack has two rows of teeth cut horizontally in its outer edges every 86mm. *Pilatus Railway*

The track was solidly built, being carried on stone blocks fitted together. The sleepers were bolted down with sling bolts which bound the masonry of the road-bed and the iron superstructure into one solid mass. *Pilatus Railway*

Wheelbase 12ft 0in
Total Heating Surface 226sq ft
Grate Area 4.09sq ft
Boiler Pressure 12 atmospheres
Water in the boiler 1069lbs
Water in the tank 1763lbs
Fuel 770lbs
Weight of the carriage body 2425lbs

Weight of the engine 6½ tons
Weight of the complete vehicle with 35 persons 10½ tons
Tractive effort 5½ tons
Mean speed 65yds/min, or 2.2mph
Radius of curves 80 metres

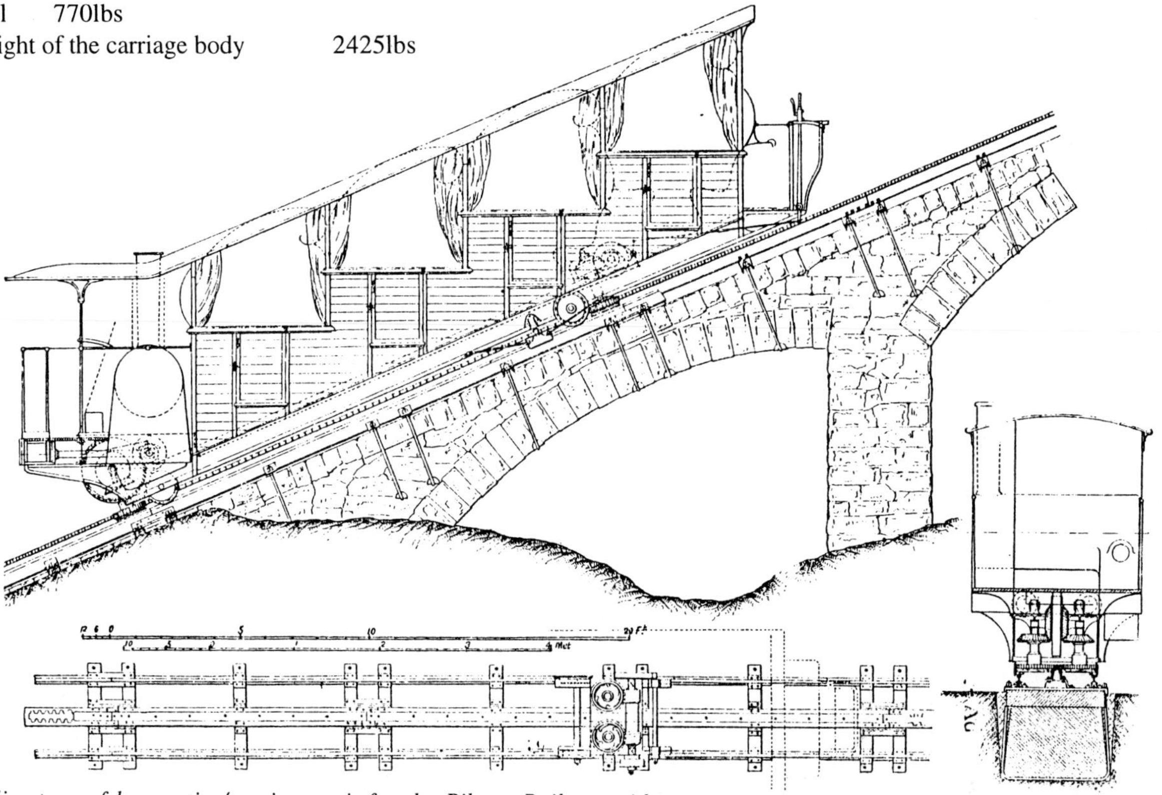

Earlier type of locomotive/carriage unit for the Pilatus Railway with cylinders at the front and beneath the water tank.

"Engineering May 13, 1887"

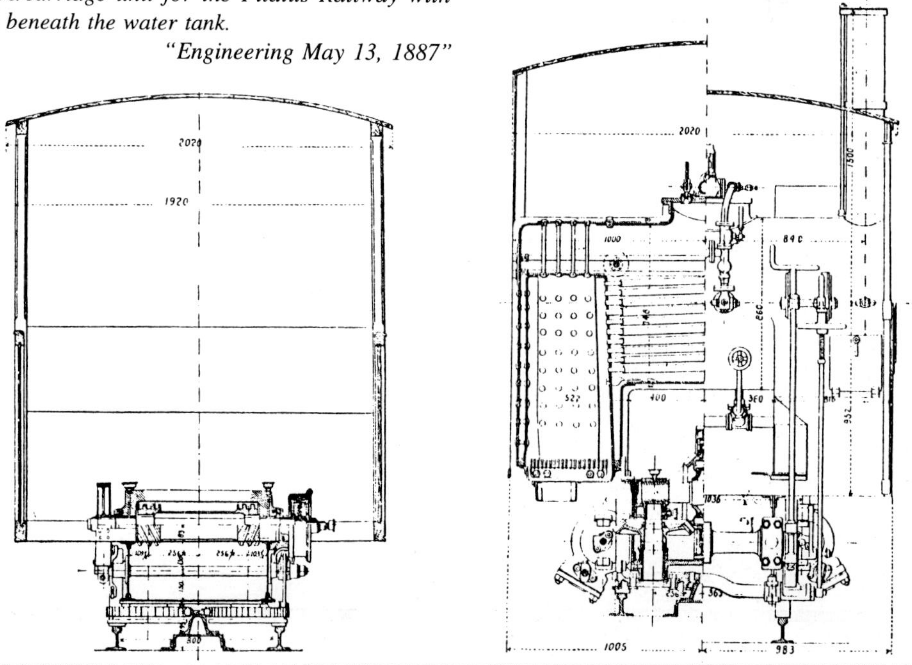

This combined locomotive and carriage was the Swiss industry showpiece at the 1889 Paris Exhibition. It was purchased by the Pilatus Railway. Note the cylinder position beneath the front of the carriage. Earlier locomotive/carriage units had the cylinders at the front end beneath the water tank - see drawing on the previous page.
"Engineering November 1 1889"

A Steam Carriage poses for its photograph when new 1888/9.
SLM, Winterthur

This drawing was published in a paper "Rack Railway Locomotives of the Swiss Mountain Railways" by T.Weber and S.Abt of SLM, Winterthur and intended to be read at the July 1911 Zürich meeting of the Institution of Mechanical Engineers. It depicts a locomotive carriage similar to that shown below, but having a platform at the top end for the conductor.

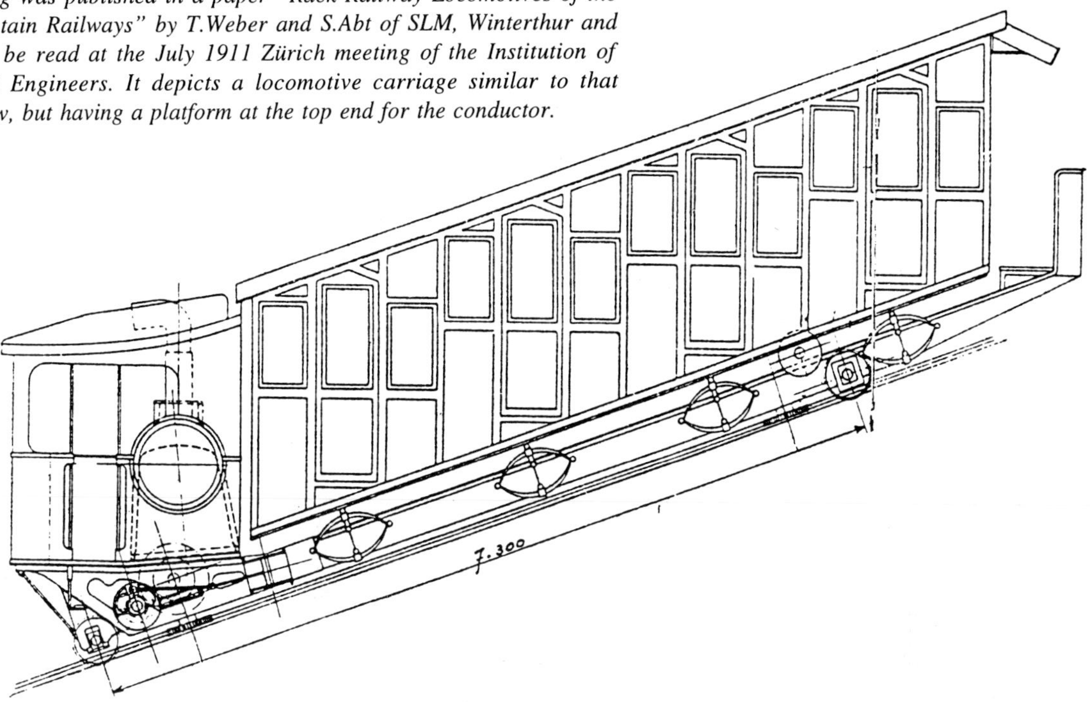

Steam Carriage No.5 when new in 1888. Note the stepped platform. *Pilatus Railway*

Steam Carriage No.7 on the Wolfort viaduct just before entering the Wolfort tunnel. This unit was displayed at the World Fair in 1889 as "a brilliant new Swiss construction". In the steam carriages the drive was mounted on the carrying axle on the valley side, while the pair of pinions on the mountain side are used only for braking. Apart from an automatic locking device the unit has two friction brakes and a compressed air-brake for the downhill journey.
Pilatus Railway

Ten steam rail carriages were built(No's 1-10)between 1886 and 1900, with a slightly heavier(No.11)in 1909:

No.	Builder	Works No.	Year	
1	SLM	451	1886	Superheated 1910/1
2	SLM	464	1887	Superheated 1910/1
3	SLM	465	1887	
4	SLM	512	1888	
5	SLM	513	1888	
6	SLM	514	1888	Superheated 1930
7	SLM	561	1889	
8	SLM	562	1889	Superheated 1930
9	SLM	563	1889	
10	SLM	1309	1900	
11	SLM	1983	1909	Superheated from new

No's 9 and 10 are thought to still exist - these were rebuilt from the components of withdrawn vehicles. No.9 was used as a service vehicle, whilst No.10 was loaned to the Deutsche Museum, Munich.

Engraving from "The Mt.Pilatus Railway" by J.Hardmeyer(Orell, Füssli & Co., Zürich)circa 1885.

Car No.21 at Alpnachstad base terminus on 12 June 1956. Observe the stepped platform built this way due to the steep incline. *P.J.Kelley*

During 1905 the first electrification project was suggested for the Pilatus railway but this was not proceeded with due to the excessive cost. Part of the existing steam coach fleet was upgraded when two units were fitted with superheaters.

The Pilatus Bahn was electrified in 1937 at 1550 volts dc using single railcars with stepped windows. The platform at Alpnachstad consists, because of its inclincation, of a flight of steps and similarly the electric motor coaches are in step formation. Passengers are then seated on the level on the steep Pilatus gradients - a feature common on funiculars but not on rack railways. At Alpnachstad motor coaches descending are transferred to the ascending track by means of an electrically worked traverser which moves the coaches sideways from one track to the other. The use of a traverser section makes complicated point-work unnecessary. Leaving Alpnachstad the Pilatus Railway climbs through meadows and woods, crossing the 75ft stone arch across the Wolfort ravine. A short tunnel and the motor coach is on the steep slopes of the Risleten. More short tunnels brings the train to the mountain pasture of the Aemsigen Alp where, half way up the ascent, is a station and electric traverser where ascending and descending trains can pass each other. In steam days locomotives replenished their water tanks at this point but when electrification was completed this stop was no longer necessary and in consequence the journey time was reduced from 70mins to 30mins up and 40mins down. From the mid-way halt the journey becomes more spectacular, the line passing through a number of short tunnels cut out of limestone projections, running on a shelf blasted out of the face of a sheer precipice. The summit station lies at a point 6778ft above sea level.

Today the Pilatus Railway is operated by electric motor coaches fitted with two pinions, one running on each side of the original Locher rack. During the mid-1970s the rolling stock comprised: 8 1937 vintage motorcoaches of type Bhe ½(2 axles, one powered), one 1967 unit, and one dual purpose vehicle, 1 departmental vehicle fitted with rack. All built to operate at no more than 7.45mph.

On Mount Pilatus, the steepest rack railway in the world with a maximum gradient of 1 in 2.08. *Pilatus Railway*

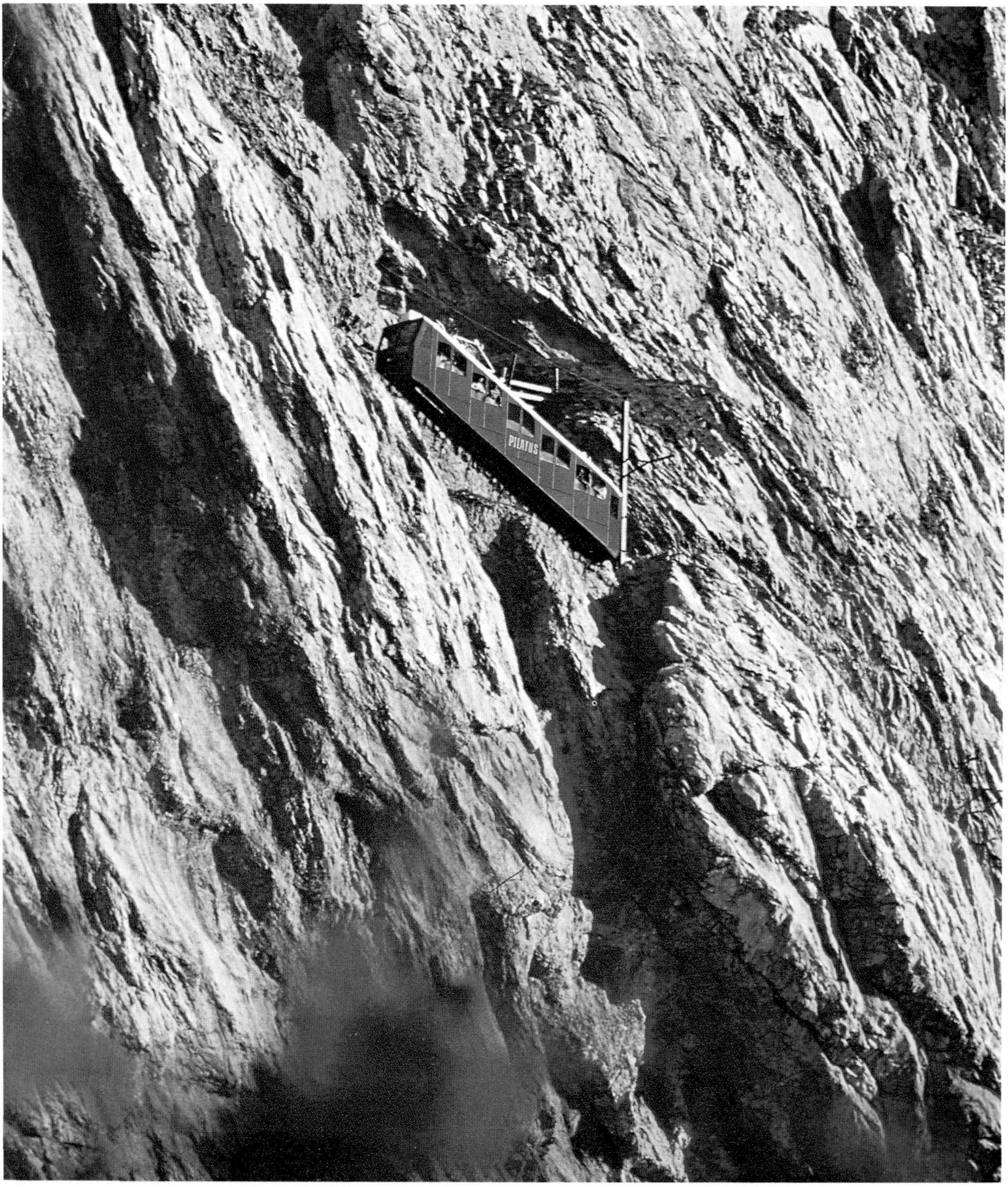

Train ascending Mount Pilatus taken from the previous train on 25 May 1954. P.J.Kelley

(Pilatus Railway No's 21-30)

Road No	Type	Builder	Year	Seats	Tonnes	Kw
21	Motor Coach	SLM/MFO	1937	40	9.65	155
22	Motor Coach	SLM/MFO	1937	40	9.65	155
23	Motor Coach	SLM/MFO	1937	40	9.65	155
24	Motor Coach	SLM/MFO	1937	40	9.65	155
25	Motor Coach	SLM/MFO	1937	40	9.65	155
26	Motor Coach	SLM/MFO	1937	40	9.65	155
27	Motor Coach	SLM/MFO	1937	40	9.65	155
28	Motor Coach	SLM/MFO	1937	40	9.65	155
29*	Motor Coach	SLM/MFO	1962	40	9.6	155
30	Motor Coach	SLM/MFO	1967	40	10.5	175

In addition there were several deparmental vehicles.

SLM - Schweizerische Lokomotiv und Maschinenfabrik, Winterthur.
MFO - Maschinenfabrik Oerlikon, Zürich.
* - Conversion to and from a passenger coach to a freight unit could be carried out within 2½hours by changing the body.

On the Amsigenalp 4430ft high and in the middle of the 2.85 mile long railway line is a crossing with two traversers. The rail sections were moved into position by means of hand cranks. *P.J.Kelley top, Pilatus Railway bottom*

Swiss ingeniousness. This traverser moves into the third dimension - on the upper surface it links the main rail with the one branch, on the lower surface with the other. Pilatus Railway

A modern-day photograph of Pilatus Car No.28 as it approaches the traverser. The pantograph is lowered so presumably the photograph was specially posed for railway publicity purposes.
Pilatus Railway

The vista from Mount Pilatus. Pilatus Railway

Facts About The Pilatus Rack and Pinion Railway - (from official sources)

Total Length(horizontal)	4270metres
Length of the sloping plane	4618metres
Length of line	4.3km
Gauge	80cm
Stations(2)	Upper terminus altitude 2070metres
	Lower terminus altitude 441 metres
Maximum grade of 48%	over 1130metres or 26% of its length
Curves	on 1610metres or 38% of its length
Smallest radius	30metres
Tunnels	7, with a total length of 333metres -
	Wolfort tunnel - 40metres long
	Two Spycher tunnels 47metres and 101metres
	Four tunnels on the Esel 9 to 50metres long
Avalanche shelters	3, with a total length of 120metres
Bridges and viaducts	23, with a total length of 229metres
Turn out track	1, on the Amsigen Alp - 1350metres elevation
Traverser	6, and 2 rail reversers
Construction started	April 1886

Railway opened	4 June 1889 with steam coaches 15 May 1937 with electric motor coaches
Ascent time	Steam coach 70min, Electric motor coach 30min
Descent time	Steam coach 90min, Electric motor coach 40min

This most interesting of all the mountain railways around Luzern was soon carrying a large number of passengers:-

Years	Steam coaches	Motor coaches	No.of Seats	Passengers - Annual Average
1889-1899	9	-	288	34,461
1900-1910	10	-	320	46,181
1911-1936	11	-	352	33,471
1937-1939	2	8	384	81,081
1940-1946	2	8	384	48,880
1947-1955	1	8	320	146,964
1956-1966	1	9	360	186,512
1967-1974	1	10	360-400	249,438

The Pilatus Railway was built to ensure that one stretch was always completed before the next was begun. Wolfort Ravine here pictured. Of special interest are the two steam locomotive/carriage units with flat bodies instead of carriage bodies, used in construction work.
Pilatus Railway

BRUNNEN MORSCHACH AXENSTEIN BAHN

At Brunnen, on the Gotthard line, one could up to 1969, change for the 1 metre gauge railway up to Axenstein, the purpose of this little railway was to transport visitors from Brunnen up to the summer resorts of Morschach and Axenstein at an altitude of 2000-2400feet. The line opened on 1 August 1905 with a length of 1.27 miles and the type of rack used was Strub. The mean gradient was 1 in 8, the maximum gradient 1 in 5.8.

The line climbed 879ft with curves of 262ft radius. It was electrified from the start and was 3-phase with two contact wires. The locomotives were connected to the coaches on Rowan's system. These units had only one driving wheel powered by two 80hp polyphase motors by means of double transmitting gear. The trailing carrying axle was provided with a brake rack-wheel, and it and the driving rack-wheel were both braked. On both up and down journeys a safety grip was used, in addition to which the brake-wheels were fitted with guide flanges in order to provide greater security against the wheels mounting the rails.

Apparently Queen Victoria said "This is the most beautiful spot I met with on my journey through Switzerland".

Closure was effected on 29 March 1969.

Car No.4 was photographed at the summit station on the Brunnen Morschach Axenstein Bahn.
P.J.Kelley

DRAHTSEILBAHN AUF DEN SONNENBERG BEI LUZERN

This 2754ft long, 1 metre gauge electric powered funicular railway was opened in 1902 with a steepest gradient of 43%(1 in 2.3). It had a total ascent of 689ft.

This undated postcard photograph shows part of the Sonnenberg Funicular Railway and gives some impression of its gradient - 1 in 2.3 in places.
Card produced by Gebr.Wehrli, Kilchberg-Zürich
P.J.Kelley collection

3 NARROW GAUGE MOUNTAIN RAILWAYS AROUND INTERLAKEN

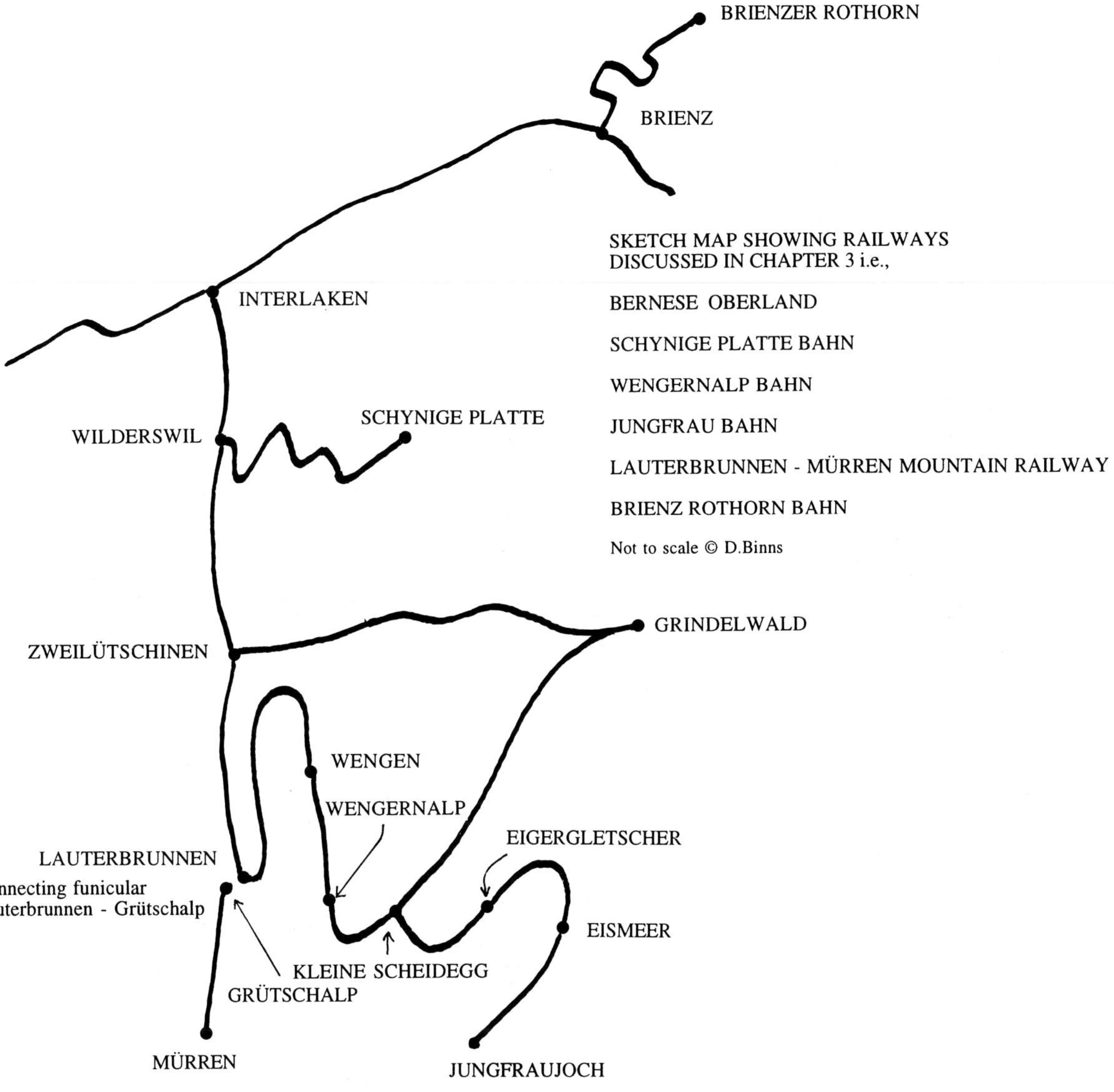

Interlaken, as the name suggests, is situated between Lake Brienz and Lake Thun. There are two stations - Interlaken West and Interlaken Ost. The latter is where the Lötschberg standard gauge route from Thun, the 1metre gauge Berner Oberland line and the 1metre gauge Brünig line all meet.

The railways of the Jungfrau region are under common management and comprise an electrified network of mountain railways with an operating length of more than 40 miles, modernised in recent years and now developed into an efficient transport system using modern rolling stock. This system includes the following companies:-

BERNESE OBERLAND RAILWAYS(BOB).
Rack/Adhesion Railway. Opened 1890. Routes - Interlaken Ost(1860ft)to Lauterbrunnen(2612ft), and Grindelwald(3393ft). Total length 14.6 miles. Gauge 1 metre. Gradients up to 1 in 8.3.

SCHYNIGE PLATTE RAILWAY
Rack Railway. Opened in 1893. Acquired by BOB in 1895. Route - Wilderswil(1916ft)to Schynige Platte(6454ft). Length 4.5 miles. Gauge 800mm. Gradients up to 1 in 4.

LAUTERBRÜNNEN - MÜRREN MOUNTAIN RAILWAY(BLM).
Funicular/adhesion railway. Opened 1891. Routes - Funicular, Lauterbrünnen(2612ft) - Grütschalp(4879ft), Adhesion railway Grütschalp(4879ft)to Mürren(5361ft). Total length 3.5miles. Gauge 1 metre. Funicular gradients up to 1 in 1.6.

MÜRREN - ALLMENDHUBEL FUNICULAR(SMA).
Opened 1912. Route - Mürren(5414ft) - Allmendhubel(6273ft). Length 587yards. Gauge 1 metre. Gradients up to 1 in 1.6.

WENGERNALP RAILWAY(WAB).
Rack Railway opened in 1893. Routes Lauterbrünnen (2612ft) to Wengen(4180ft), to Wengernalp(6145ft), to Klein Scheidegg(6762 ft). Also Grindelwald(3393ft), to Kleine Scheidegg(6762ft). Total length11.8miles. Longest single stretch of rack railway in Switzerland. Gauge 800mm. Gradients up to 1 in 4.

JUNGFRAU RAILWAY(JB).
Rack Railway. Section Kleine Scheidegg(6762ft), to Eigergletscher(7612ft). Opened 1898.Eigergletscher (7612ft)to Eigerwand(9400ft), in 1903. Eigerwand (9400ft), to Eismeer(10,368ft) in 1905, and Eismeer (10,368ft), to Jungfraujoch(11,333ft) - the highest railway station in Europe, opened in 1912. Length 5.8miles. Gauge 1 metre. Gradients up to 1 in 4. Length of tunnel from Eigergletscher(7612ft) to Jungfraujoch (11,333ft)4.4miles.

INTERLAKEN-HARDER FUNICULAR(HB).
Opened 1908. Route - Interlaken(1860ft), to Harder Kulm(4337ft). Length 1530yards. Gauge 1 metre. Gradients up to 1 in 1.5.

BERNESE OBERLAND BAHNEN.
The 1 metre gauge Bernese Oberland Bahnen runs from Interlaken Ost to Zweilütschinen where it divides into two branches, one to Lauterbrünnen and a second to Grindelwald. The total length is 14.6 miles out of which 3 miles was fitted with the Riggenbach rack. There are two rack sections on each branch with gradients averaging between 1 in 8½ and 1 in 11. On the adhesion sections the maximum gradient was 1 in 40. Single line throughout the line now handles heavy traffic with Grindelwald and Lauterbrünnen trains running as one from Interlaken to Zweilütschinen where they split. Popularly known as the 'Valley Railways' the BOB opened on 1 September 1890 and was steam operated.

Interlaken Ost station exterior on 2 June 1955 on a very wet day. The single-decker bus in the station yard is from Hotel Victoria Jungfrau.
P.J.Kelley

The line formed an economically important link between Interlaken and the two large valley communities from which there are connections to the highest regions of the Bernese Oberland. The BOB was converted to electric operation opening on 17 March 1914. This was followed by a renovation programme to the 1500v d.c. system between 1948 and 1952 at a cost of 3.7 million Swiss Francs.

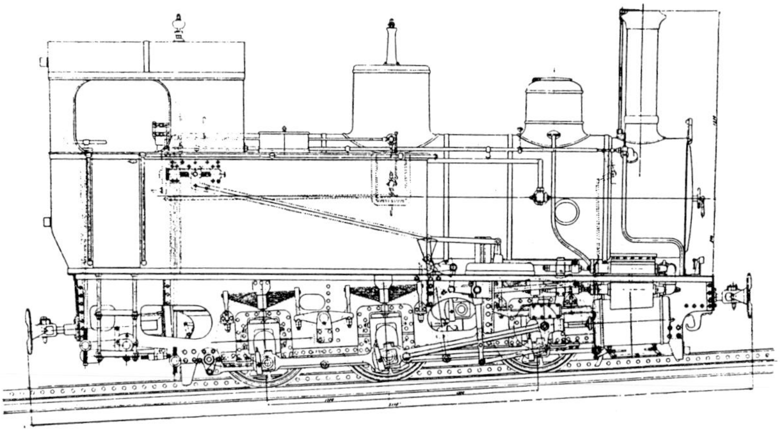

The original BOB rack/adhesion tank locomotive illustrated by this drawing was six-coupled and had 4 cylinders with seperate driving gear for adhesion and for rack working. The inner pair of cylinders transmitted power to an intermediate shaft with pinion gearing directly in the toothed driving rack-wheel. A loose braking rack-wheel was placed on the leading adhesion axle. Each pair of cylinders had a seperate regulator but both were operated by one controlling screw. Both the rack and the adhesion mechanisms were controlled by an air repression brake, in addition to which both rack wheels were also provided with seperate hand-brakes. The third hand-brake which acted on all the adhesion driving wheels was used as a shunting brake. The locomotive was provided with a Klose continuous steam-brake for braking the train.

D.Binns collection

This small rack/adhesion locomotive "Eiger" had been built in 1893 as SLM Works No.797 and became No.11 in the BOB list.

D.Binns collection

A typical Swiss scene. A steam rack locomotive descending on the Bernese Oberland Bahnen with the Jungfrau in the centre background. Note the load of three coaches and a van. From a colour postcard by R.Gabler, Interlaken.

P.J.Kelley collection

No.26 HGe 3/3-1(SLM Works No. 2370/1914)on the 09.28am train from Interlaken Ost at Wilderswil on 27 May 1955. Trains run to both Lauterbrunnen and Grindelwald splitting at Zweilutschinen. P.J.Kelley

A BOB train at Grindelwald awaits departure to Interlaken Ost on 7 July 1950. Locomotive No.22 was built by SLM in 1914.
Ian G.T.Duncan

The 10.30am train from Interlaken Ost approaching Zweilutschinen on 29 May 1955, hauled by HGe 3/3-1 No.27. Built SLM 1914, Works No.2371(?).

P.J.Kelley

Wilderswil on 1 June 1955 with railcar BCFhe 4/4 No.303 on an Interlaken train.

P.J.Kelley

SCHYNIGE PLATTE BAHN

Some 3 miles south of Interlaken, in the heart of the Jungfrau Region, the Schynige Platte 6454ft provides a popular vantage point where an all-round view of the Bernese high alps is possible. Passengers arrive from Interlaken Ost 1860ft and at Wilderswil 1916ft on the Bernese Oberland Bahnen, change trains for the Schynige Platte Bahn. This is an 800mm gauge Riggenbach rack line 4½miles long which climbs more than 4500ft by a 1 in 4 ruling gradient. Opened on 14 June 1893, it was taken over by the BOB in 1895, with electrification at 1500v d.c. taking place in 1914. Next to the summit station is the entrance to the Alpine Botanical Garden with more than 500 varieties of plants.

In the days before the Wengernalpbahn was modified locomotives and rolling stock were exchanged between the summer operation of the Schynige Platte Bahn and the winter sports area of the Wengernalpbahn. When the latters old stock became surplus the best of it was transferred to the SPB and assorted liveries were evident with a mixture of BOB brown, WAB green and SPB red and cream. One steam locomotive is used in winter for maintenance when the overhead wires are dismantled, and of course for rail specials in summer.

A rack locomotive pushes a single carriage on the Schynige Platte Bahn around the turn of the century. In the background the Eiger, the Mönch and the Jungfrau. From a colour card produced by Photographie R.Gabler, Interlaken.
P.J.Kelley collection

Electric locomotive He2/2 No.12(SLM Works No.2347 of 1914)was seen at Schynige Platte on 27 May 1955.
P.J.Kelley

The Bernese Oberland Bahnen purchased ten 3-axle rack/adhesion locomotives numbered 1-10. The locomotive illustrated was No.6 of that Company. The Schynige Platte Bahn had been taken over by the BOB in 1895 and No.6 was photographed at Wilderswil on the Schynige Platte Bahn with a newly repainted carriage in BOB livery. The Schynige Platte Bahn had six rack tanks of its own and these carried No's 1-6, being built by SLM, Winterthur - No.1 Works No.692 of 1891, No.2 Works No.713 of 1892, No's 3/4 Works No's 800/1 of 1893 and No's 5/6, Works No's 881/2 of 1894.

C.J.Walker collection

The original No.1(SLM Works No.692/1891)was photographed out of use at Wilderswil on 27 May 1955. *P.J.Kelley*

Class He2/2 No.14 was a product of SLM(Works No.2349/1914)and was photographed heading the 09.37am train to the summit about to leave Wilderswil on 27 May 1955. *P.J.Kelley*

WENGERNALPBAHN

A typical Swiss wintry scene on the Wengernalpbahn with the Wetterhorn behind. From a black and white card by Phototypie Co., Neuchâtel. *C.J.Walker collection*

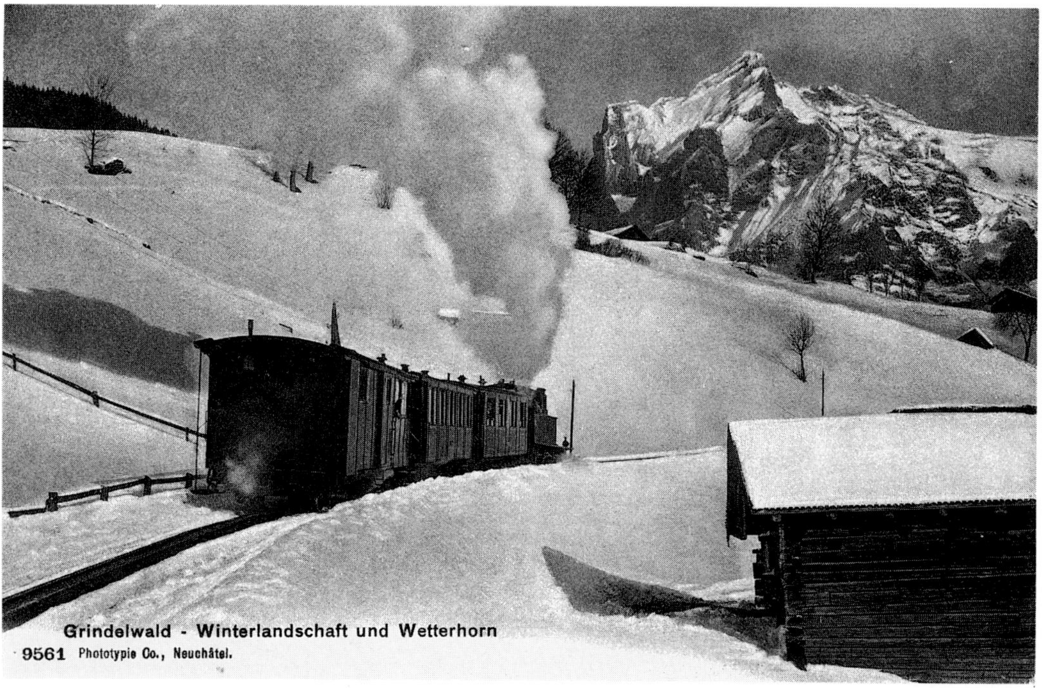

The Wengernalpbahn leads up to the Jungfraubahn. It runs from both Lauterbrünnen and Grindelwald to the junction at Kleine Scheidegg. The section between Lauterbrünnen and Scheidegg opened on 20 June 1893 and was electrified on 3 July 1909, being originally steam operated. A second line starting from Grindelwald to Scheidegg opened for electric working on 24 June 1910 providing a quicker and more reliable ascent especially in winter. The section Lauterbrünnen - Scheidegg was 6.51 miles long climbing 4147ft, whilst that from Grindelwald to Scheidegg was 5.37 miles in length and climbed 3665ft.

During 1948-51 an extensive renovation programme was carried out including the purchase of 7 high-speed rail motor cars and the building of a shunt-back on Kleine Scheidegg, which together cost some 3million Swiss Francs. In addition, a second rotary plough was acquired and in Lauterbrünnen and Grindelwald new locomotive sheds were built. During the 1950s rolling stock consisted of 15 electric locomotives built 1909/29, 7 high-speed rail cars built between 1948 and 1954, 2 rotary ploughs, 41 passenger cars, 31 goods vehicles and 3 ordinary snow ploughs.

A locomotive from the series 1-14 was photo-graphed on the Wengernalpbahn with the Wetterhorn behind the train. Note the conductor on the end platform footstep. From a black and white card by Verlag Photographie R. Gabler, Interlaken. C.J.Walker collection

The Wengernalpbahn took delivery of 14 11/3 Abt rack tanks from SLM, Winterthur in the years 1891-1898. The type is illustrated by this photograph. These carried Road No's 1-14 and SLM Works No's 690/1 of 1891, 749/750 of 1892, 802-805 of 1893, 919-921 of 1895, 977 of 1896 and 1420/3 of 1898.

SLM, Winterthur

With the Jungfrau in the distance a Wengernalpbahn train climbs upwards. The locomotive is unidentified but different to No's 1-14. From a colour card by R.Gabler, Interlaken. P.J.Kelley collection

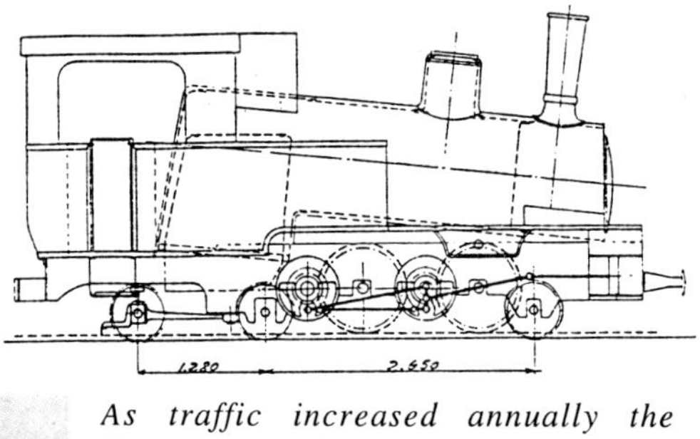

As traffic increased annually the Winterthur works of SLM were asked to provide heavier locomotives and in 1904 built a new type for this railway with a tractive power of about 10.8 tons(11,000kg)against 6.3 tons (6,500kg)of the earlier types. The new design had three carrying axles, the trailing one being of the Bissel type. One locomotive(no.31)was built in 1904(SLM Works No.1588), with a second(No.32)in 1906 (Works No.1730). These are illustrated by drawing and photograph.

C.J.Walker collection

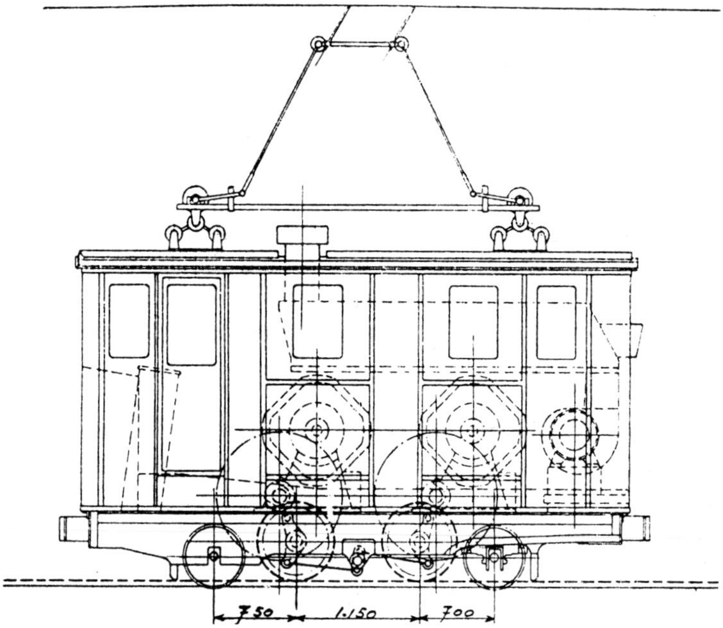

The Wengernalp Railway started to use elctric power in June 1909 and within a year or so had ten locomotives of 300hp each. These were generally of the same construction as those of the Gornergrat and Jungfrau railways. Of note is the fact that the Wengernalp electric locomotives were the first constructed for the narrow gauge of 800mm. This caused difficulties to SLM in designing the transmission and in the arrangement of the brakes. Each locomotive had two series continuous current 150hp motors, with full power being capable of continuous use. When running down-grade braking was by the ordinary method of short-circuiting.

D.Binns collection

Electric locomotive No.59 was photographed on the Wengernalp Bahn not in winter as might be thought, but in June 1949. *H.E.Meyer*

He2/2 No.58 built in 1929, was photographed having just arrived at Kleine Scheidegg on 30 May 1955.

P.J.Kelley

JUNGFRAU BAHN

On 27 August 1893 the Zürich industrialist Adolf Guyer-Zeller climbed the Schilthorn near Mürren with his daughter. On the way down he stood lost in admiration before the size and majesty of the giant trio, the Eiger, the Mönch, and the Jungfrau. Suddenly he caught sight of clouds of steam rising into the air in the direction of the Wengernalp - it was a train of the(then)newly opened Wengernalp Railway slowly climbing to Kleine Scheidegg. Guyer-Zeller remembered the earlier schemes for the construction of a Jungfrau railway and at that moment his own great plan took shape in his mind. The line was to start at Kleine Scheidegg and be linked up with the already existing Wengernalp Railway. The track would be laid in the direction of the Eigergletscher, from this point it would enter the Eiger by means of a steadily climbing tunnel, loop inside the mountain, proceed beneath the Mönch and the Jungfraujoch, and spiral to a point immediately below the summit, which would be reached by a 200ft lift.

On 21 December 1894 Guyer-Zeller was granted authorisation to build the 1metre gauge Jungfraujoch railway and on 27 July 1896 work was begun at Kleine Scheidegg, the junction station with the Wengernalpbahn at 6762ft above sea-level. The individual stations were opened in stages: Eigergletscher in 1898, Eigerwand in 1903, and Eismeer in 1905 10,368ft at which point the estimated cost of 7½million Swiss Francs had been exceeded. A decision was then made to site the upper terminus on the saddle between the Jungfrau 13,642ft and the Mönch 13,449ft. The terminus station at 11,333ft is the highest in Europe.

The line from Eismeer to the summit was built differently to the original plan and up to 500yards before the Jungfraujoch station the tunnel was constructed on an easy grade of 1 in 15.8 so that at the beginning trains could operate on this section by adhesion alone. The remaining sections of the tunnel were built at an incline of 1 in 4. The inadequacies of this mixed rack/adhesion system were corrected in 1951 when the adhesion section was also equipped with a rack- rail throughout its length. The section between Kleine Scheidegg and Eismeer has a difference in level of 3580ft with a length of 3.6miles by a gradient of 1 in 4. Where the Jungfraubahn is in open cutting the curves have a radius of 328ft, curves in tunnel being of 656ft radius and curves leading into points have a radius of 262½ft. Strub rack gear was first applied on the Jungfraubahn and 3-phase current used.

Electric power was used from the start at 7000v. 3-phase at 40 cycles which was stepped down to a working voltage of 650v. Power stations to provide current were built at Lauterbrünnen and at Lütschental.

The Jungfraujoch terminus - still the highest station in Europe - was opened on 1 August 1912 after 16 years of constructing the 5.76mile(9.27km)railway. The 4.4mile(7km)long tunnel through the Eiger and Mönch alone occupied 14 years.

The Jungfrau Railway is still a masterpiece of Swiss railway construction

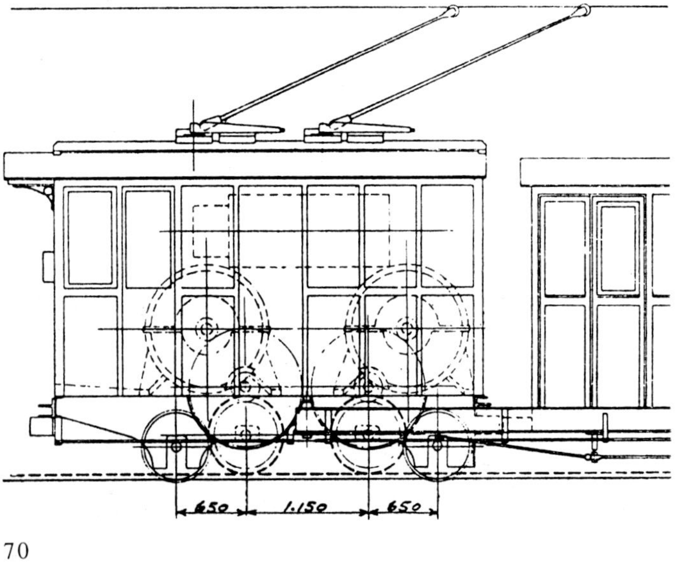

Twelve electric rack locomotives were delivered to the Jungfrau Railway between 1898 and 1929. These had two motors of 120-165hp at 800rpm. Two passenger coaches with accommodation for 40 passengers each are pushed by one locomotive over grades as steep as 1 in 4 in places. The locomotive illustrated is of the same construction as those supplied to the Gornergrat Bahn but its performance was somewhat higher. Train speed was 4.65mph. When running downhill braking was controlled by means of an electric resistance cooled by a fan. The motors then worked as ordinary generators due to a special change in their connections, and current thus generated was transformed into heat. They had a maximum tractive power of 6.8 tons. *D.Binns collection*

Opposite Page: Original rolling stock consisted of the twelve Rowan units, i.e., a locomotive with a passenger carriage carried on the locomotive frame at one end and a bogie at the other. Rowan unit No.5, building date believed to be 1898, at Kleine Scheidegg on 30 May 1955. *P.J.Kelley*

1 Jungfraujoch Station
2 Hotel Berghaus/Terrace
3 Lift to 4th floor
4 Restaurant
5 Footpath to Plateau
6 Ice Palace
7 Entrance to Sphinx Tunnel
8 Tourist Hotel
9 International Research Institute
10 Sphinx Tunnel
11 Sphinxlift
12 Sphinx Terraces 11,723 ft.
13 Exit from Sphinx Tunnel
14 Polar dogs

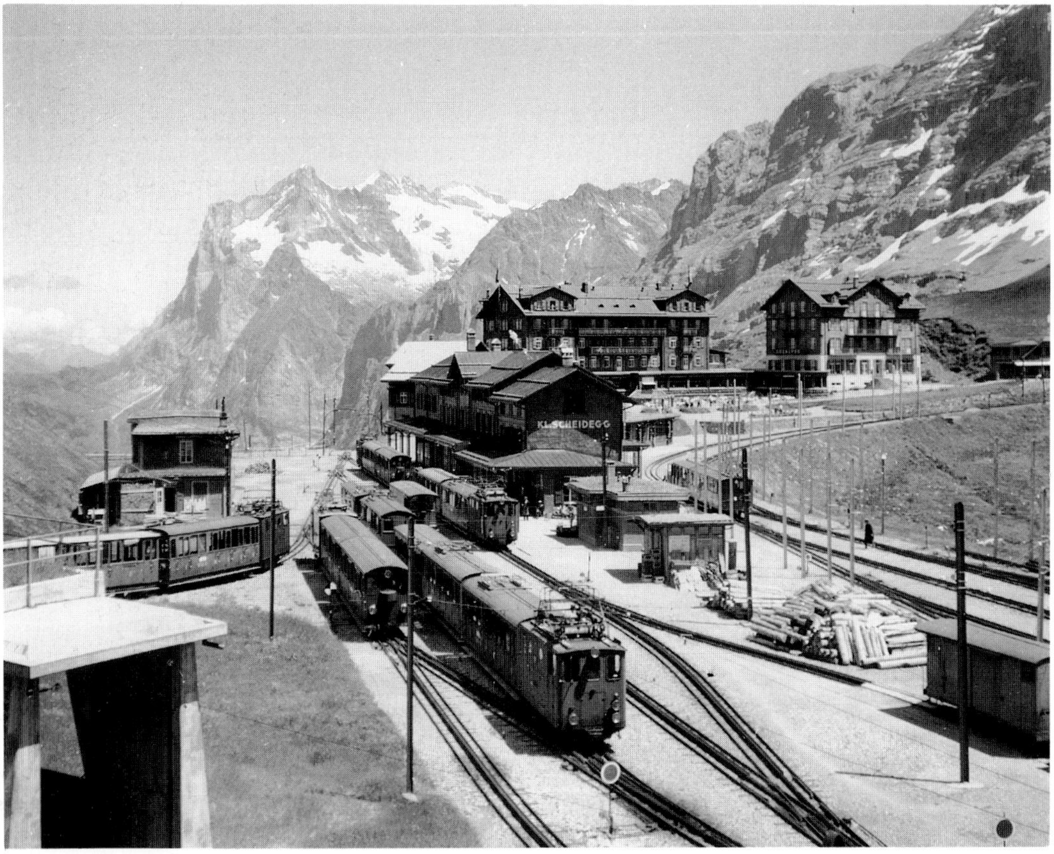
KL.SCHEIDEGG

Kleine Scheidegg, summer 1949. This mid-summer photograph makes one shudder at the thought of winter and what it might bring!. *H.E.Meyer*

Opposite top: Kleine Scheidegg showing both the 800mm gauge Wengernalpbahn and the 1 metre gauge Jungfraubahn on 30 May 1955. In the foreground are two Wengernalp locomotives, No's 55 and 59. *P.J.Kelley*

Opposite bottom: Kleine Scheidegg on 8 July 1950. A Wengernalpbahn train from Lauterbrunnen can be seen on the curve on the left of this picture. The four tracks in the centre contain Wengernalpbahn trains. The main station buildings are in the centre behind these trains and the line curving off to the right is the Jungfrau Bahn. *Ian G.T.Duncan*

More recent power on the Jungfraubahn in the shape of BDhe 2/4 railcar No.201(built by SLM, Works No.4113/1954)at Kleine Scheidegg on 30 May 1955. Ten of these railcars were built between 1955/1960-4. *P.J.Kelley*

Stone monument at Interlaken to 'Dem Schopfer der Jungfraubahn' translated 'The creator of the Jungfrau Railway A.D.Guyer-Zeller 1839-1899'. Photographed on 26 May 1955. *P.J.Kelley*

LAUTERBRÜNNEN-MÜRREN
MOUNTAIN RAILWAY

The Bergbahn Lauterbrünnen-Mürren opened on 14 August 1891. It consisted of two parts - a 0.8 mile funicular railway from Lauterbrünnen to Grütschalp with an average grade of 1 in 8 and a maximum of 1 in 6. It has a halfway passing loop and the funicular is operated by two cars. Originally operated by water counterweights, problems were encountered with freezing-up so conversion to electric power was undertaken in time for the 1901/2 season. Each of the cars has a platform at its upper end to carry boxes of supplies for the village of Mürren(which is traffic-less) - goods being transferred at Grütschalp by a rack-operated forklift unit to a wagon attached to the rear of a waiting railcar. The funicular had been renovated during 1948-50 with a complete renewal of the cable sections and a new driving mechanism. The old rails, together with the rack, which was formerly needed for braking purposes, were replaced and a new cable was installed.

The second section was a 3.5 mile long 1 metre gauge cliff top adhesion railway from Grütschalp to Mürren which runs on a ledge overlooking the Eiger, Jungfrau and Mönch. Electrically operated from the start using tram type vehicles which were replaced by Rowan units in 1903, then again in 1913 by two 4-axle electric railcars, with a further example added to stock in 1925. There were also two platform trucks for goods and a snowplough. One of the 1913 railcars - Be 2/4 No.11 - has been restored to its original livery for special use. Three new Be 4/4 railcars No's 21-23 were placed in service in 1967 having been hauled up the funicular line before reaching the railway. Maximum gradient on the railway was 1 in 20 with power being provided at 525v d.c. There is also an intermediate station and passing loop at Winteregg.

A cable railway - the Mürren-Allmendhubel opened in 1912 and came under the same management.

Railcar BD2/4 No.11 built 1913, en-route between Grutschalp and Mürren on 1 June 1955. P.J.Kelley

Railcar BD2/4 No.13 built 1913, en-route between Grutschalp and Mürren on 1 June 1955. P.J.Kelley

Trestle Bridge between Grutschalp and Mürren on 1 June 1955. P.J.Kelley

A four-wheeled electric locomotive was photographed prior to 1905 hauling a single carriage on the Mürrenbahn with the Eiger, Mönch and Jungfrau behind. The carriage is interesting being a double bogie vehicle with open end platforms, open centre section and short closed sections either side. From a card by Künzli-Tobler, Zurich - postmarked 21 November 1905.

P.J.Kelley collection

A modern view along the Lauterbrunnen-Mürren line with the Breithorn behind.

Jungfrau Railway

DRAHTSEILBAHN INTERLAKEN-HARDER KULM

The Valley station of the Drahtseilbahn Interlaken-Harder Kulm is only 3 minutes from Interlaken Ost Railway station. This 1metre gauge funicular railway opened on 15 May 1908 climbing 2418ft in its total length of 4056ft by 1 in 1.56 maximum gradients. Various figures have been published having regard to the length of the line but 4056ft was confirmed from official sources. Trains start from both lower and upper terminals and need 16 minutes to complete their journeys. The Harder Kulm lies at 4337ft and affords sweeping views down to Interlaken and the Lakes of Thun and Brienz. A panorama of snow covered peaks centres on the Eiger, Mönch and Jungfrau.

Car No.2 was photographed from Car No.1 on 2 June 1955.
P.J.Kelley

This car was photographed on the Interlaken - Harder Kulm funicular circa 1920. From a postcard by Edition Photoglub, Zurich. Card inscribed "Grand Restaurant Harderkulm (1325m) . ob Interlaken, A.Beugger, Hotel Gotthard, Interlaken".
P.J.Kelley collection

DRAHTSEILBAHN INTERLAKEN HEIMWEHFLUH

Five minutes walk from Interlaken Hauptbahnhof there is the base station of the Drahtseilbahn Interlaken Heimwehfluh funicular which opened on 21 July 1906. The length of this 1metre gauge line is 610ft and the total ascent of 334ft is made at a gradient of 1 in 1.6. Journey time is 2½minutes. Apart from the view at the summit there is a large model railway and restaurant to be sampled, the model railway being built in 'O' gauge in 1951.

Car No.2 was photographed on 29 May 1955 beginning the descent from the upper terminus. *P.J.Kelley*

STEFFISBURG THUN INTERLAKEN STRASSENBAHN

Between Interlaken and Thun there used to be a tramway called the Steffisburg Thun Interlaken Strassenbahn. The line was 16¼ miles in length and of 1metre gauge. It opened from Steffisburg to Oberhofen on 10 October 1913; to Beatenbucht on 24 December 1913 and to Interlaken on 20 June 1914. The section between Interlaken and Beatenbucht closed on 18 December 1939, from Beatenbucht and Merligen on 31 January 1952 and from Merligen to Thun on 18 August 1952. The rest of the line was closed on 31 May 1958, the service being continued by trolleybuses and motorbuses.

Tram No.1 at Thun on 31 May 1955. The initials on the car side looks like 'STJ' but the 'J' is actually an 'I' in the old style German script being used. The three cars on the right appear to be trailers.
P.J.Kelley

BRIENZ ROTHORN BAHN

Brienz - Rothorn Bahn rack tank No.6 was photographed near the summit in July 1939. Card by Photoglub-Wehrli & Vouga & Co., AG, Zurich.
C.J.Walker collection

Along the Brünig line on the shores of Lake Brienz is the lovely village of Brienz where one finds the Brienz Rothorn Bahn, a 4.7mile 800mm gauge mountain railway using the Abt system of rack throughout. Opened in June 1892 after two years of construction the line climbs to the summit at Rothorn 7380ft by a ruling gradient of 1 in 4, the total ascent being 5515ft. The BRB suffered financial problems, some brought about by the first world war which resulted in closure from 1915 to 1930. It re-opened in 1931 and despite a slight setback at the beginning of the second world war, is now a successful tourist attraction. The journey takes about one hour in each direction. The BRB is still steam operated and in 1992 took delivery of one new steam locomotive built by SLM, followed in 1996 by two more.

The Brienz-Rothorn Bahn started with four rack locomotives purchased from SLM - No's 1/2 Works No's 688/9 of 1891 and No's 3/4 Works No's 719/720 in 1892. No.3 was photographed at Brienz on 9 July 1950.
Ian G.T.Duncan

No.6 at Brienz 9 July 1950. Built by SLM, Works No.3610/1936.
Ian G.T.Duncan

No.6 was photographed soon after leaving Brienz on the ascent on 9 July 1950.
Ian G.T.Duncan

Train descending with No.7 using steam as a brake, on 28 May 1955. *P.J.Kelley*

Station at Brienz on 28 May 1955. The sign 'Betrieb eröffnet means 'service open'. The line only runs in the summer months and 28 May was the first day of the summer service for 1955. Class H2/3 No.7. Built by SLM, Works No.3611/1936. *P.J.Kelley*

Train at summit station on 28 May 1955 with No.7 in charge. *P.J.Kelley*

Locomotive No.7 at Summit station. Driver washing his hands. *P.J.Kelley*

View of track showing double teeth of Abt rack system. Also note the thickness of the snow even though it is late May. *P.J.Kelley*

THE NEW H 2/3 STEAM RACK LOCOMOTIVES

4

After an interval of some 40 years the Swiss Locomotive & Machine Works(SLM), Winterthur again entered the steam locomotive market when it started construction of new H2/3 steam rack locomotives. Initially, three prototypes were delivered in 1992 one each, to the Brienz - Rothorn Railway, the Montreux-Glion-Rochers de Naye Railway, and the Austrian Federal Railways.

If the new locomotives were to stand any chance of success, building to an old design was out of the question, but to limit the technical risk a reference type was needed. For this two Brienz-Rothornbahn locomotives No's 6 and 7(ordered from SLM in 1933 and 1936)seemed best suited. Drawings of this type were held by SLM but not the calculation data.

Diesel locomotives are not appreciated on mountain rack railways and a representative poll revealed that 79% preferred steam haulage. This suggested that in the interests of economy steam operation should not be sacrificed but more economical operation should be the order - more fare paying passengers - less personnel.

Only the appearance is reminiscent of the old steam locomotives. The new ones can be operated by a driver only; one-man operation being essential to compete economically with diesel or electric traction. One-man operation is made easier by the fact that trains are pushed, i.e., the locomotive is at the bottom end. Whilst ascending, line observation is the job of the conductor riding in the front car of the train so leaving the driver to concentrate on his locomotive. When descending the driver has to observe the track but of course the boiler requires no attention. Various improvements were incorporated into the new locomotives ensuring that the driver is not overtaxed by his dual responsibility. These include 1) oil-firing. In comparison with manual coal firing, oil-fuelling already saves a lot of work. This is made easier with the installation of a newly developed compound governor enabling the firing rate to be controlled by one hand. 2) Boiler feed by running pump - a mechanically driven feed pump for feeding the boiler while travelling. The feed rate is controlled by a throttle valve. 3) Mechanical central lubrication. The driver does not have to worry about lubrication whilst travelling, additional lubrication is provided in the depot at intervals. 4) So-called 'vigilance pedals' are provided for safety.

Mountain railway traffic depends very much on the weather, a sudden bright spell after a period of rain often brings with it a large number of passengers who then cannot be moved owing to lack of locomotives under steam. To improve the operational readiness of the new steam locomotives SLM has designed an external electrical pre-heating device enabling a cold steam locomotive to be put under steam and held ready for operation unattended. An oil-fired locomotive is thus ready for service in about ten minutes. On a fine day mountain rack railway locomotives operate only 9-10 hours, the rest of the time they stand in the depot. To save energy and personnel, the boiler has efficient insulation, enabling the locomotive to be kept under steam overnight so that it is ready for immediate service. The boiler is welded throughout. Two pop-type safety valves are mounted on the dome. The regulator is actuated laterally and can be operated from a standing or seated position. When compared to BRB No's 6 and 7, the drive has been revised with the welded cylinder block now underneath the smokebox. The steam engine is a superheated twin unit with Heusinger valve gear. The frame is also welded. The downhill carrying axle is of the Bissel type. Three brake systems are incorporated into the new locomotives - 1) A Riggenbach counter-pressure brake in which the cylinders act as a compressor, the valve gear being set against the direction of travel so that air is drawn in and compressed. In the process heat is generated, which can be converted into steam by injecting cooling water. The braking action can be controlled from the downhill side of the cab by means of a throttle valve. 2) There are two mechanical stopping brake systems, the first is a spring-operated brake actuated by compressed air and distributed throughout the train. Provided on the locomotive are two spring-operated brake cylinders which each act on a brake drum with two brake pad carriers by way of individual brake linkages. This system is operated by the driver from a brake valve on the drivers desk on the downhill side of the cab. 3) An additional brake system is concentrated on the locomotive and is able to bring the whole train to a halt without the help of the carriage brakes. This is in the form of a band-brake operated by a manual spindle acting on two brake drums of the crankshaft. The hand braking crank is located on the drivers desk on the downhill side of the cab.

The new locomotives are equipped with a modern electronic safety and emergency brake control system. Because 24v/1kw steam turbo-generators are no longer being manufactured anywhere in the world, batteries had to be adapted for the locomotives current supply. These are charged by way of a mechanically driven alternator whilst travelling, or charging can be effected by an ordinary outside battery charger. The batteries are easily accessible from outside being located in drawers under the drivers' cab on the left. Apart from the alternator and batteries, all electrical and electronic equipment is fitted in the rear wall of the cab, enabling the steam part and the electricity to be segregated. Principal current consumers are the electrically driven compressor and three solenoid valves, plus various automatic circuit breakers, control relays and lamps.

In traditional steam operation one of the problems has always been the time needed to raise steam, a cold engine needing hours to achieve this. The electrical pre-heater developed by SLM offers the following possibilities:- 1)Unfired, unattended heat-up of a cold locomotive to working pressure. 2)A heated locomotive can be kept warm or under pressure unattended. 3)The boiler can be filled without opening wash-holes or flanges. 4) Remote controlled switch-on by telephone. Boiler water is taken from the boiler and flows by gravity to a hot water circulation pump. This pumps water through the electrical heater(where it is heated)back into the boiler. The forced circulation causes extremely uniform heating, because the entire boiler is heated from the water-side and therefore has the same temperature everywhere - unlike conventional warming up, which heats the firebox and tubes first while the outer firebox and boiler barrel are still cold. The electrical pre-heater warms up the boiler water slowly to a temperature set on a thermostat. The time needed to warm up a cold locomotive to a pressure of 10 bar depends on(1)the heating capacity of the pre-heater, (2)the water content of the locomotive boiler(3)effectiveness of the boiler insulation, (4)tightness of air dampers and chimney cover. The new pre-heater for steam rack locomotives is rated at 25kw. With a cold boiler this means 12-16 hours to bring a boiler to working pressure. A cold locomotive pre-heated overnight is then ready for immediate service next morning. Before moving the locomotive, the pre-heater must be detatched from the boiler, switching-off and disconnecting the two flexible hoses being a five minute job. If the pre-heater is used to keep warm a locomotive under pressure, the required temperature must be set on the thermostat.

One-man operation and the strict regulations laid down in the Execution Rules of the Railway Ordinance(AB-EBV)required particular attention to comprehensive safety provisions including vigilance pedals with quick and slow action, an overspeed trip and a roll-down safeguard. the vigilance pedals are in the cab on the uphill and downhill sides. When travelling uphill the uphill pedal must be pressed. When descending, the downhill one is pressed because their signals are used to evaluate the direction of travel for the roll-down safeguard. All monitoring functions, speed and distance displays and recording are provided by a 'Teloc 2000 S' unit by way of a central module in a 19in pull-out rack located on the downhill side of the cab. The two-channel speed measuring signal is picked up on the specially serrated brake-drum of the crankshaft on the left by two proximity switches.

Most oil-fired steam locomotives burn heavy fuel oil(Bunker C). For the new steam rack locomotives this was ruled out for various reasons. Heavy fuel oil needs warming for filling-up and firing, necessitating heating coils which means more weight and extra energy. The high sulphur content is not environmentally friendly and is detrimental to boiler life due to corrosion. Now-a-days heavy fuel oil is used only by major industry and is difficult to obtain in Swiss tourist resorts, whereas there is good distribution network for 'extra-light(EL)'fuel oil as used in domestic central heating. Accordingly EL fuel oil was specified. This was a new concept which was worked out by SLM and Sonvico.

The fact that the last steam locomotives had been built by SLM in 1952, and the abundance of technical innovations needed to bring the traditional technology to the present level, made a works trial seem advisable. The idea of employing a second steam locomotive as a brake locomotive made possible an attractive low-cost test stand. On two inclinable ramps provided with rackless tracks, the two locomotives were set up parallel and after dismantling the bar couplers they were joined by means of a cardan shaft on the intermediate gear. Owing to the staggered production there was only one locomotive available at first and on 5 February 1992 Brienz-Rothorn Bahn locomotive No.12(Works No.5456)was put on the test stand, the instruments checked and the boiler heated using the electrical pre-heater. After blowing-out the boiler and steam engine, the pilot burners, auxilliary blower, injector and mechanical brakes were tested. On 10 February the new locomotive was steamed and run, with immediate success. With mechanical braking it was possible to run under load a little, enabling the first electronically measured indicator diagrams to be recorded.

The completion of locomotive 999.201 for the OBB

on 13 March 1992 meant that this could be used as a brake locomotive. Even under load there were few problems. The principal task on the load test stand was matching the blast pipe to the oil firing. The measured results were much better than had been calculated. After a few measuring tests at the power needed on the Brienzer Rothorn(about 200kw)the load trials with the BRB locomotive had to be concluded. It had been intended to run upto the performance limit of the locomotive(around 300kw)on the test stand but had this been undertaken No.12 would not have made the centenary celebrations. After concluding load tests the BRB locomotive was painted and transported to Brienz on 18 May 1992. This event - the arrival of a new steam locomotive after 56 years - provided an excuse for a village festival.

First track tests in the station area went off without problems. Braking trials revealed that both mechanical stopping brakes retarded too much. This was soon made right and once the brake retardation valves met the regulations, track trials could begin. Acceptance by the Federal Bureau of Transport was passed with distinction on 5 June 1992 whereupon the locomotive was officially handed over for service. Speedy and suprisingly uncomplicated commissioning enabled the locomotive to be handed over to the railway for operation before the centenary celebration. The commissioning of the new steam locomotive and the world-wide publicity effect associated with it no doubt contributed to the new passenger record achieved(up 37% on the previous record).

On 2 July 1992 locomotive No.1 of the Montreux-Glion-Rochers de Naye Railway was unloaded at Montreux and warmed up with the electrical pre-heater. Next morning the first run under load took place with Acceptance by the Federal Transport Bureau on 10 July. Nine days after delivery the new locomotive performed its first commercial trip and with great reliability proceeded to work the scheduled six weekend uphill runs not to mention 28 relief trains as well.

Experience has shown that the new steam rack locomotives have acquitted themselves well and the requirements laid down in the specification have been met or exceeded. Compared with other prototype motive power the commissioning time was short and these locomotives were able to enter commercial operation within a short period following delivery. Most of the disadvantages of traditional steam traction have been eliminated and in operational readiness, availability and personnel costs they can match diesel and electric traction. Fuel costs are minimal, maintenance costs have been good and environmental nuisance is no longer a problem with the new oil-fired locomotives.

Four years on, four successful years as regards the new SLM steam rack locomotives, it is good to report that the Brienz - Rothorn Bahn ordered two more and these No's 14 and 15 were officially taken into service on 13 August 1996. On that day No's 14 and 15 were readied to haul seperate trains carrying invited guests(shareholders, employees of the BRB, and local dignitaries), up to the Rothorn while No.12(the 1992 new locomotive)was prepared to take the service train.

A view inside the SLM works at Winterthur showing the gearing arrangement on one of the new steam rack locomotives. *SLM, Winterthur*

Finance for No's 14 and 15 was provided for by an increase in the share capital and BRB have stated that these two new steam locomotives will guarantee steam operations on the line for the next decade. It is intended long term to replace the four diesel hydrostatic locomotives built between 1973 and 1987. In addition to No's 14 and 15, SLM are supplying three more units to the Austrian Federal Railways.

The scene is set for the SLM to sell more of these highly efficient steam rack locomotives ..... well done to the designer Roger Waller and his crew at Winterthur.

In addition to new construction at Winterthur, SLM have re-furbished their first ever steam rack locomotive and the following press release dated March 1996 is reproduced:-

"Sulzer Technology Corporation
Corporate Press Office
8401 Winterthur
Winterthur, March 1996 Switzerland

First SLM steam loco back in service.

After repair work lasting for a year or so, the first steam loco ever made by Swiss Locomotive and Machine Works Ltd., has been handed back to the Vitznau-Rigi Railway. Staff at SLM and the Rigi Railway have breathed new life into this old piece from the Swiss Transport Museum in Luzern. Loco No.7 is over 120 years old. After a spectacular journey by lake transport from Luzern to Vitznau, it will be steaming along the line daily from 21 May to early October.

The veteran steam loco was taken from the Swiss Transport Museum in Luzern to Winterthur on 7 March 1995 for restoration and repair in preparation for this year's 125th anniversary of the Vitznau-Rigi Railway and the SLM. At the SLM works, it was dismantled into hundreds of components which were then compared with original plans dating from 1871/73. The result was astonishing: despite the advanced age and long years of service, a great many parts were still fit for use.

Dedicated staff.

Teams of volunteers were formed at SLM and the Rigi Railway to specialise in the overhaul of various components. 20 or so employees in Winterthur joined up to handle their share of the work which took no less than 1200 hours of hard effort. Workshop apprentices were also involved. "The dedication shown by SLM staff

Two of the new 1990s H2/3 rack locomotives under test in the Winterthur Works of SLM. On 5 February 1992 Brienz-Rothorn Bahn No.12 was put on the test stand and the instruments checked and the boiler heated using the elctrical pre-heater. On 10 February the new locomotive was steamed and run with immediate success. On 13 March 1992 No.999.201 for the OBB was completed and was used as a brake locomotive. The main task on the load test stand was matching the blast pipe to the oil firing. *SLM, Winterthur*

in performing this far from routine work is a source of great satsfaction to us. It is evidence of the high level of identification of our locomotive specialists with products of former times and of the pride which they take in their work", is the satisfied comment of SLM Manager, Richard Kummrow.

The steam loco which was taken out of service in 1937 is to be recommissioned as far as possible in its original condition. time had of course taken its toll of some parts. "For instance, we had to redesign and rebuild the whole steam boiler system; that was no easy task, especially as the original drawings were no longer complete", explains Werner Müller, project manager at SLM. "A new drive was also needed as the original version had seized up. The original wooden brakes no longer satisfied today's more stringent railway legislation and had to be redesigned".

Spectacular voyage.

Despite modifications to satisfy modern engineering standards, the "Riggenbach schnapps distillery", as Loco No.7 was popularly known because of its vertical boiler, will be largely in the original condition of its early days when it sets out on its jubilee trips. A few more weeks are still needed for the finishing touches. After a spectacular voyage by lake from Luzern to Vitznau, reproducing the original delivery voyage, trials and training trips will still have to be made followed by acceptance by the Swiss Federal Office of Transport. At long last, on 21 May 1996, Loco No.7, pulling the nostalgic presentation coach B2 dating from 1871, will be back in service between Rigi Staffel and Rigi Kulm. It will continue to run on this route at a maximum speed of 7.5km/h with 120 horse power until October. Under the terms of the contract with the Swiss Transport Museum, it must then be restored to its original condition and put on show again as a museum piece".

Railway trials of the rebuilt and restored vertical boiler locomotive No.7 of the Vitznau - Rigi Bahn were photographed in May 1996. *Heide duss-bürgi, courtesy SLM, Winterthur*